TRAINED
TO KILL

TRAINED TO KILL

THE INSIDE STORY OF CIA PLOTS AGAINST CASTRO, KENNEDY, AND CHE

ANTONIO VECIANA

WITH CARLOS HARRISON

FOREWORD BY DAVID TALBOT

Skyhorse Publishing

Skyhorse Publishing books may be purchased in bulk at special discounts for sales promotion, corporate gifts, fund-raising, or educational purposes. Special editions can also be created to specifications. For details, contact the Special Sales Department, Skyhorse Publishing, 307 West 36th Street, 11th Floor, New York, NY 10018 or info@skyhorsepublishing.com.

Skyhorse® and Skyhorse Publishing® are registered trademarks of Skyhorse Publishing, Inc.®, a Delaware corporation.

Visit our website at www.skyhorsepublishing.com.
10 9 8 7 6 5 4 3 2 1

Library of Congress Cataloging-in-Publication Data is available on file.

Cover design by Brian Peterson

Print ISBN: 978-1-5107-6947-2
Ebook ISBN: 978-1-5107-1357-4

Printed in the United States of America

CONTENTS

FOREWORD

"**SOMEONE WOULD HAVE** talked." That's the argument the lone gunman crowd has always fallen back on whenever confronted by the growing evidence of a conspiracy in the assassination of President John F. Kennedy. The truth is, numerous people with knowledge about the dark operation in Dallas more than half a century ago *have* talked. But few in Washington or in the mainstream media were listening.

The list of those who talked and were either ignored or silenced begins with JFK intimates who rode with him in the fateful Dallas motorcade, including First Lady Jacqueline Kennedy and White House aides Kenneth O'Donnell and Dave Powers—all of whom immediately reported that the president's limousine was caught in a lethal cross fire that day in Dealey Plaza. Jack Ruby, the Mafia hit man who conveniently muzzled the self-proclaimed "patsy" Lee Harvey Oswald, also began to talk to government investigators—until he was shut up.

The line of eyewitnesses and co-conspirators who had much to say about the Kennedy assassination stretches into the current century, with CIA officer E. Howard Hunt, leader of the Watergate burglary team, confessing late in his life to playing at least a peripheral role in the Kennedy assassination conspiracy, along with such other notorious agency operatives as William Harvey and David Morales.

Now we have the remarkable, revelatory memoir of Antonio Veciana, a legendary leader of the anti-Castro underground whose shadowy exploits were sponsored by the CIA. Robert F. Kennedy, who served as his brother's attorney general, became convinced immediately after the gunfire in Dallas that the plot against JFK had grown out of the CIA's secretive Cuba operation. In *Trained to Kill*, Veciana finally and definitively confirms that RFK's suspicions were true. Veciana recounts that shortly before President Kennedy's assassination, he witnessed his CIA handler, David Atlee Phillips—a rising star in the agency's Latin America division—meeting with Oswald in Dallas.

This is a mind-blowing revelation because it's the only credible eyewitness account to connect Oswald—the accused assassin and likely scapegoat—directly to an important CIA official. Phillips emerged as a key suspect in Kennedy's murder during the House Select Committee on Assassinations hearings in the 1970s. He squirmed and stonewalled and chain-smoked under interrogation by committee members and staff.

Phillips was no rogue agent—he was a prized member of the core team built by CIA spymaster Allen Dulles to fight the spread of Communism and left-wing movements in South America and the Caribbean. He consistently received promotions and commendations throughout his twenty-five-year career at the CIA, which in addition to his involvement in the agency's Castro assassination plots also included his leadership of the covert operation against Chilean President Salvador Allende, who died during a CIA-instigated coup in 1973. After retiring in 1975, when the agency was under sharp attack from Congress and the press for its subversive excesses, Phillips founded the CIA's first overt lobbying group, the Association of Former Intelligence Officers.

Veciana too led a colorful and violent life, and his memoir is filled not just with gripping insights into the Kennedy assassination, but with inside stories about the relentless crusade to kill Fidel Castro and to track down the other hero of the Cuban Revolution, Ernesto "Che" Guevara. Veciana's intimate portraits of these charismatic men and their murderous antagonists in the CIA and the Cuban underground put the reader squarely inside some of the most dramatic episodes of twentieth-century history.

Starting off his career in Havana as a mild-mannered banker and devoted family man, Veciana found himself sucked into the whirlwind of events that placed Castro's Cuba in the bull's-eye of U.S. imperialism. Though he remained a dedicated anti-Communist partisan through most of his life, Veciana had the integrity and courage to finally question the ruthless methods and mentality of his CIA sponsors. His growing disenchantment with the agency put not only his own life but that of his family at risk, and for years he wrestled with the decision to go public about the Lee Harvey Oswald-David Atlee Phillips connection.

Now, in old age, Antonio Veciana has finally unburdened himself of the secrets of his life. His story sheds light on some of the darkest corners of American history. *Trained to Kill* should be read by all of those who wonder and worry about our country's incessant imperial adventures and how they have tragically undermined our democracy.

—David Talbot,
February 2017

PREFACE

I DON'T KNOW who killed John Kennedy. I know who wanted to. He was with the CIA. He introduced me to Lee Harvey Oswald. In Dallas. Two months before JFK died.

By then, he had already taught me to be an agent, in Cuba. By then, I had already tried to kill Fidel Castro, the first time.

The man I knew as Maurice Bishop supplied the training. He supplied the money. He supplied the weapons.

I found the men. I found the place. I failed.

But I didn't give up. Neither did Bishop.

The CIA has repeatedly denied that one of its highest-ranking officials used the cover name of Maurice Bishop. Confessing that David Atlee Phillips used that pseudonym would connect the agency—or at least one of its most important functionaries—with Oswald. And that, by extension, would link it to Kennedy's death.

The very fact that they do deny it proves to me they know something. There's no need for a cover-up when you're innocent.

David Atlee Phillips rose to be the CIA's chief of Western Hemisphere operations. He hadn't reached that level yet when I met him, but he was clearly powerful. He could order Castro's death and supply the means to do it.

When it came time to spirit me out of Cuba, he provided me with a job, working for the United States government in Bolivia. But still, even there, my target was Castro.

Again, the man I knew as Bishop—and years later by his real name—supplied the money. He supplied the intelligence. But I have no idea how he would've reacted if I had been caught when I smuggled the weapons he provided into Chile. I didn't tell him that I had piled my three children and my wife into the car for the trip. For them it was a vacation. For me it was cover—what border guard would ever suspect a family on a road trip? With three small children squealing excitedly, and a young wife in the passenger seat.

That was the first time I unthinkingly—perhaps selfishly, or blindly—put my family's lives at risk in my zeal to kill Castro. It wasn't the last.

Bishop knew I was responsible for the arsons that destroyed some of Havana's best-known department stores, which led to something I could never forgive myself for, the death of an innocent mother of two. Bishop knew I was the one responsible for sparking the mass exodus of thousands of Cuban children known as "Operation Pedro Pan"—disguised as orphans, and with the help of the Catholic Church. Bishop knew I came close to collapsing Cuba's economy with a rumor campaign meant to sow panic.

And even though I know there are those who suspect it was Bishop, not Castro, who hired the hit man who tried to put the bullet in my head, and even though I know it might have been Bishop, not Castro, who set me up and sent me to prison, I defended him. When I was called before the House committee reinvestigating the Kennedy assassination, I said nothing. When I met him face-to-face in the hall outside a CIA luncheon, I said nothing.

Now I will.

I have been written about. I have been questioned. This is the first time I tell the story for myself. The whole story.

Why now? In the past, I knew that Castro, and others, wouldn't hesitate to do away with their enemies by putting a bomb under their car. I was well aware of what could happen as I traveled with my wife and children. Now I'm old. My wife is gone. My children are grown. I have survived cancer and a heart attack. Now I can reveal the truth about my double life.

My name is Antonio Veciana. I am an accountant by training, a banker and a businessman by trade. Some call me a patriot. Some call me a terrorist. Only one knew I was a spy, with a single mission—destroy Castro. My CIA handler, the man I knew as Maurice Bishop. The man whom congressional investigators later identified as master spy David Atlee Phillips. The man whom I saw meeting with Lee Harvey Oswald in Dallas.

chapter 1
A BAZOOKA IN THE NIGHT

THE MAN WITH the bazooka watched and waited. The apartment he was in looked out over the plaza where the crowd was gathered. Among the people, he knew, were some of his confederates, about twenty, with pistols and hand grenades. He knew none of them by name. They had never met. Had he been in the crowd himself, under the sparkling stars of the Havana sky, he could have stood right next to one of the gunmen and not known it. It was done that way on purpose. For safety. You can't reveal what you don't know.

They were there to kill Castro. They were there because of me.

It was October 5, 1961. Cuban President Osvaldo Dorticós had just returned from a tour of Iron Curtain countries. His itinerary bore witness to Cuba's newfound prominence in the pantheon of global players. He had been to Belgrade to attend the inaugural Summit of the Non-Aligned Nations, a group formed largely on the vision of leaders who stand among history's giants—India's first prime minister, Jawaharlal Nehru; Indonesia's first president, Sukarno; Egypt's Gamal Abdel Nasser; and Yugoslavia's Josip Tito—and consisting of countries that supposedly stood separate from either of the superpowers. Of course, Dorticós almost immediately demonstrated how ludicrous that presumption of independence really was by heading to Moscow for a ten-day visit and a meeting with Nikita Khrushchev. Then he flew directly from there to meet Mao in Red China.

Returning to Havana after his high-profile globetrotting, Dorticós was greeted by Castro at José Martí International Airport. That night, they were due to address a welcoming rally from the north terrace of the Presidential Palace. It was a victory lap. And it was an opportunity. Apartment 8-A, on the eighth floor of the building at No. 29 Avenida de las Misiones, sat exactly 120 yards away from the palace, in the corner of the top floor closest to it, with a clear and unobstructed view of that north terrace. I know, because that's why I had rented it almost a full year before.

The building was a modernist gem, a Mondrian rectangle with a brightly colored façade patterned in distinctive squares and repeated rectangles. But, as they always say with real estate, what made it most valuable was location, location, location.

The three-bedroom apartment had come available because the American man who owned it was going back to the United States. Bishop told me how lucky I was to have found it, and I agreed. What he didn't tell me was that the man was a spy and the apartment had been a meeting place for CIA operatives. I don't know if he knew that the Cubans knew that. I don't know if he knew they had been watching the place. They had even seen David Atlee Phillips, the man I knew as Bishop, there.

I didn't know any of that when I got my mother-in-law to sign the lease and moved her in, in October 1960. I didn't know that Castro operatives were still watching now, a year later, and had seen me come there twenty days earlier, on September 15, to go over final details of the plan with the core group of assassins. There was no sign of the surveillance the night before, either, when I had come to the apartment at 11:00 p.m., carrying a long, gift-wrapped package with a lamp jutting out of the end.

I had seen uniformed men on the street, as was increasingly common in Havana in those days, but none of them seemed to pay any special attention to me. And none of them stopped me to check the package.

If they had, they would have discovered a standard U.S. military issue M20 shoulder-mounted antitank rocket launcher—known to everyone the world over as a bazooka. Its 3.5-inch warhead could supposedly pierce a three-inch armor plate and stop a rolling tank at four hundred yards. That was well over what we needed.

If all went according to plan, Fidel and Dorticós would stand in plain view on that terrace just a football field away, unmoving and unprotected, surrounded by top cabinet members and government officials. With a little luck, our attack would not just eliminate Fidel, it would take out a significant chunk of Cuba's revolutionary hierarchy. And, knowing Fidel's predilection for long-windedness, our shooter would have hours to aim and wait for just the right shot, if he wanted.

The regime's increasingly repressive security apparatus didn't stop me as I carried what appeared to be a gift-wrapped lamp, and they didn't pay any particular attention to the middle-aged woman with me. They didn't follow us as we stepped into the rectangular building facing El Prado, the wide, tree-lined walk that led from the Presidential Palace to the statue of Máximo Gómez. Gómez was a national hero, the brilliant military commander who invented the "machete charge" that sparked terror in the hearts of the Spanish troops during Cuba's fight for independence. His statue overlooked the entrance to Havana Bay. None of that was really on the minds of the lovers sneaking kisses and surreptitious touches in the long shadows beneath the oak trees lining the path. They were oblivious to the other shadowy intrigue unfolding nearby.

Maybe the police and the regime's watchmen were more interested in catching a glimpse of the lovers on the lane, or too busy cadging cigarettes off the passersby they could intimidate. Whatever the reason, they didn't join us as we stepped into the elevator and rode up the eight floors, or as we walked down the hall to the apartment the woman with me called home.

Inside, the team of assassins was already waiting. They had been since September 25, quietly waiting for Dorticós's return. When I arrived nine days later with the bazooka, they were stir-crazy and anxious. But I had the weapon they had been waiting for, and news—Dorticós had finally arrived in Havana, and he and Fidel would be addressing a crowd in the plaza the following evening, at the end of the workday.

The plan had been months in the making. Bishop knew. In fact, he had convinced me to call off an earlier attempt, in midsummer, when the first man in space, Russian cosmonaut Yuri Gagarin, triumphantly toured Havana after touching back down on Earth.

The idea then had been similar. We had known Gagarin was coming for weeks. After the Soviet Union stunned the world with its unexpected launch and put the first human into outer space, the Communists surely would want to thumb their noses at the United States. What better place than Cuba? Losing the tropical island that was my homeland to an openly disdainful "revolutionary" regime already served as a thorn in the yanquis' side, or lower. The embarrassingly disastrous failure of the Bay of Pigs invasion in April 1961, just days after Gagarin and his Vostok 1 spacecraft circled the Earth, only served to pour salt in the wound. Bringing the successful and photogenic young international celebrity to appear (as he later would) hugging Fidel Castro—just in time for the eighth anniversary of the uprising that gave name to the revolution—that was too delicious an opportunity for both Castro and Khrushchev to let pass.

And I knew it. So I prepared.

That was when I first started gathering weapons and moving them into the apartment my dear mother-in-law lived in.

Finding weapons in Havana in the wake of the Bay of Pigs was not hard. Despite its desire to eliminate any internal threats, Castro's regime was still in its infancy. It did not have a KGB or the capacity— hardly even the knowledge—for such repressive machinery. It was learning rapidly, and the nascent G2 apparatus that would eventually eradicate nearly every perceived and potential enemy was already starting to spread its tentacles into every corner of Cuban life. But this was early on. Castro's power still came more from popular support than it did from totalitarian control. He needed to be careful not to rouse the people's suspicions or provoke their ire. Politically— and logistically—it was one thing to move against an open menace, another entirely to storm through the homes of the entire citizenry.

With Bishop's help, and using contacts I had developed with his help and on my own, I rounded up .30-caliber M1 carbines, a couple of Czech 9 mm automatic pistols, some .45-caliber Tommy guns, hand grenades, and what I thought would be perfect for what I had in mind, a 60 mm mortar.

Lacking any military experience, I expected such a powerful weapon—capable of lobbing rounds with a lethal blast radius into the midst of a gathering hundreds of yards away—would be ideal. The target, the north terrace, to me appeared to be a perfect platter serving up the highest-ranking heads of the regime.

The Presidential Palace itself was a soaring spectacle of stately excess, part fortress and part cathedral. Built in 1920, it stood as a baroque revival monument to Cuba's days of lavish affluence, when it bathed in a shower of money from the United States and, soon after, the mob. It had an arcade façade with fake Corinthian columns and towering arches, repeated like a hall of mirrors around every side. Ornate turrets stood at the corners of the rooftop, and a massive dome sat on top. It was exemplary in its somber pomp, its superfluous self-importance, its grandiose pretensions.

Most important to me, though, was that wide, flat terrace stretching over the north porte cochere. It sat under a relief of Cuba's coat of arms, shielded only by a waist-high balustrade, and it was where Fidel and his puppet president would bask regularly in the adulation of the crowd, often for hours on end.

It was perfect, I thought.

Only it wasn't.

Not with a mortar. The blast would be perfect, but the trajectory problematic.

We would have, at best, one shot. A good mortar crew could fire off many more rounds, up to thirty in a minute. But there would be no time to adjust the aim. If we missed with the first round, Castro would be able to scramble inside to safety, and our chance would be gone forever.

Plus there was the problem of the angle of fire. A mortar pitches a shell in a high arc. It's perfect for hitting targets behind walls, or in trenches. It's terrible for aiming through an apartment window at a target seven stories below. And while being barely over a hundred yards away would be an advantage for most weapons, that put us close to the minimum range of the 60 mm mortar. Overshooting the target was a very real, and troubling, possibility.

All this I would learn after I pulled together the team to carry out the operation.

At the moment, though, all I could think about was having the very clear opportunity of doing away with Castro and giving Cubans a chance to freely choose their future.

Bishop, and members of my own group, however, saw things differently. Killing Castro was one thing. Killing Yuri Gagarin, the first human in space, was another altogether. Gagarin had done nothing wrong, and he was, as the American astronauts who formed the Mercury 7 were already coming to be seen, a hero. He had gone where no human had gone. He had floated above the planet—above every other human being—and returned to tell about it. It didn't matter that the American Alan Shepard had matched his feat within a matter of days. Gagarin was, in the world's eyes, a star: our first starman.

To kill him was wrong. And, as Bishop would argue, it would be disastrous for the group responsible. It had the very real potential to spark the outrage of not only the Soviets, but also the world. He didn't say it, but he surely must have imagined the consequences if the CIA wound up linked to the killing of Gagarin. It would surely ignite an international incident and, in the already touchy reality of Cold War relations, ratchet up tensions between the United States and the Soviet Union to a dangerously precarious level.

So, no. Gagarin would not die. And neither would Castro. Not then, anyway.

Gagarin made his visit. I bided my time.

Gagarin stepped off an Ilyushin Il-18 aircraft on July 24, 1961, in what the press described as "a lashing rain"—what we in Havana called "summer." He was, as the Associated Press reported, given "a hero's welcome." Of course, a crowd was summoned, a national holiday declared. Instead of work, the people were told to gather in the plaza and show their admiration. For Gagarin. For Castro. What went unsaid, but largely understood, was that there were those—union bosses, neighborhood committee members, loyalists—who would note a person's absence. And not in a favorable way.

My Cuba was changing. Fast. Now the people fell into camps, those filled with passion and those with fear.

So they gathered in the plaza that day. A military band played the Cuban and Soviet national anthems as the smiling twenty-seven-year-old "exchanged greetings with Castro, President Osvaldo Dorticós, and the hundreds of diplomats and high officials on hand." At least, that is how the wire services would describe it.

I knew, as always, Gagarin would next visit the Presidential Palace, and, knowing Castro, it was practically inevitable that the regime would muster a crowd to cheer enthusiastically from the plaza and that Fidel would bring the world's first spaceman out for one of his agonizingly loquacious, impromptu speeches.

Mercifully, I was wrong. Castro brought Gagarin to the Presidential Palace. And they appeared on the terrace, together with Dorticós and a cluster of other dignitaries. And the gathered populace roared appreciatively. But Castro didn't speak. Not that day.

Two days later, on July 26, the eighth anniversary of the Moncada Barracks attack that gave Fidel's revolution its name, "hundreds of thousands of cheering Cubans gathered in José Martí Square." Gagarin, wearing a milk-white short-sleeved military uniform and a crisp officer's dress white hat, railed against the United States with words that were surely music to Fidel's ears.

As the Associated Press report from that day continued, Gagarin called the Cuban revolution "one of the biggest pages of history of the liberation of the Latin American continent." He said the Soviet Union "heard with indignation the news of the bandit attack by mercenaries of North American trusts" at the Bay of Pigs. And, the AP announced, he "pledged 'the armed help of the Soviet people' in what he called Cuba's fight for independence." The crowd roared.

They roared again as Fidel, wearing his customary fatigues and his by then famous unkempt beard, embraced the cosmonaut.

President Dorticós presented Gagarin with the order of "Playa Girón," a medal, the AP explained, "created only 10 days ago as the highest Cuban decoration." Already, the regime had turned the calamitous Bay of Pigs assault—"Playa Girón" to the Cubans—into a badge of honor for itself and a public relations weapon against the United States.

I watched and gritted my teeth. So did Bishop. Kennedy's refusal to send in support for the CIA-trained exiles caught on the beach during the invasion rankled him. It was, to Bishop, a betrayal he could never forgive. He grumbled about it repeatedly as spring gave way to summer, and summer gave way to fall.

By October, life had changed dramatically. I sent my wife Sira and our children into exile in Spain for their safety. I stayed behind, more determined than ever.

It had been an eventful year—in Cuba and around the world. After the Bay of Pigs invasion failed, tensions between the United States and Castro's Communist regime escalated.

The Berlin Wall went up in August.

Freedom marchers and police clashed across America's south.

I cared only about Cuba, and about ridding my country of Castro and his Communist stain.

Repression and reprisals were on the rise. And I expected only worse. Dorticós wrote the law authorizing death by firing squad against enemies of the state, and the regime showed no hesitation in using it. So, when Bishop finally said that it was clear that the only way to eliminate Communism in Cuba was to eliminate Castro, I took him at his word.

And now, Dorticós was about to give me another chance.

History may see Dorticós as Fidel's puppet, and I sometimes call him that myself. In some ways he was. But more than that, he was Fidel's pawn. Dorticós was a believer, as was, I'm convinced, El Che. That was their strength, and that was their weakness. In ways I'm sure only Fidel knows completely, they were used.

Dorticós may have seemed an unlikely president when Fidel named him to the post in July 1959. As one writer put it, "the only thing he had ever presided over before becoming Cuba's chief executive was the Cienfuegos Yacht Club." In his book *Cuba: The First Soviet Satellite in the Americas*, Daniel James called Dorticós "a curious kind of 'bourgeois' Communist which Cuba seems to have produced in some quantity."

Dorticós was born to a wealthy family in Cienfuegos, on the island's southern shore. Founded by French settlers from Bordeaux, the city is known as the Pearl of the South. It boasts an unparalleled collection of nineteenth-century architectural treasures in its downtown. For that reason, it is now recognized as a World Heritage site, with more than three hundred neoclassical buildings that went up between 1819 and 1900. It is the birthplace of the legendary Cuban singer Benny Moré and, later, of a man I would align myself with in the fight against Castro, a one-time CIA operative who I and many others are convinced was responsible for the bombing of Cubana de Aviación flight 455 and the deaths of all seventy-eight people on board, Luis Posada Carriles.

It is, in short, a place of culture and contradictions, and perhaps, then, both an unlikely and a highly suitable birthplace for a socialist attorney descended from someone who in his time was one of the richest men in the hemisphere.

Dorticós worked for a short time as a teacher, then studied law and philosophy at the University of Havana. He got his law degree in 1941, four years before Fidel began his studies there. It was there that he joined the Popular Socialist Party, which had originally been called the Cuban Communist Party, and served as secretary to its founder.

During the 1950s, Dorticós built up a prosperous law practice in his hometown and, as Daniel James would later remind us, served as commodore of the Cienfuegos Yacht Club. He was also known as a prominent fencer and an oarsman. Nonetheless, he opposed the government of Fulgencio Batista and helped provide arms and supplies to the rebel forces fighting against it. That led to his arrest in 1958, and to his exile in Mexico.

When Batista fled and Fidel took power the following New Year's Day, Dorticós returned to Cuba and was named Minister of Revolutionary Laws. It was a good choice. He was instrumental in rewriting the Cuban Constitution and in drafting the Agrarian Reform Act that nationalized cattle ranches and expropriated and redistributed large agricultural landholdings. It was Marxism at its basest—from each according to the regime's wishes, to each according to its needs.

And when Fidel's first puppet president, Manuel Urrutia, had the audacity to go against him, Dorticós was the natural choice to replace him.

On becoming president on July 17, 1959, Dorticós again showed he was a true believer in the ideals of the revolution—at least in the professed ideals. He refused to live in the Presidential Palace, and continued to live with his wife in his Havana apartment.

But the palace continued to be used for state events. And Dorticós tackled his duties as chief executive admirably. Plus, his disdain for the United States equaled Fidel's. There's no telling how long that had been the case, but he may have even come to suspect the feeling was mutual when the Bay of Pigs invasion landed on his birthday.

So the chance to prove Cuba's newfound place of importance, and its new allegiances, must surely have been welcome. It gave Dorticós—and Cuba, and Castro, of course—an opportunity to shine on the world stage. More important, and more troublesome for the United States, it gave the Revolution a chance to become a beacon for other countries in Latin America to similarly "rise up against their oppressors," i.e., the gringos.

Dorticós knew it. So did the Soviets.

And both knew the power of the press.

Dorticós primed the pump at the Summit of Non-Aligned Nations in Belgrade with what the *New York Times* called "the most violent speech heard here since the twenty-four-nation parley opened."

Capitalizing on Cuba's position as the only Latin American country with full status at the meeting, the Cuban president, the *Times* reported, "urged the conference of uncommitted countries today to condemn United States 'imperialism, colonialism and neocolonialism' in Latin America."

He "pressed for a resolution asserting that the United States was not an appropriate host country for the United Nations." Instead, he insisted, the U.N. headquarters should leave New York for "a country where human dignity is better protected." He also called on the United States to abandon its base at Guantanamo and, in a deliberate echo of Soviet interests, came out in favor of "an immediate German peace treaty 'recognizing the existence of two Germanys.'"

Dorticós got a visibly chilly reception from other representatives at the summit, but that couldn't have mattered to him. The story didn't make the front page of the *Times*, but close enough—it played as the lead story on page 3, devoted entirely to his comments.

If Tito, Nehru, and Nassar "displayed expressions of annoyance as the Cuban President attacked the United States," they were nothing compared to the grimaces that must have spread through Washington as they read the article there.

But Dorticós was just warming up.

Right after the summit, he made a visit to the Kremlin. The trip lasted ten days. The media followed his every move. The cameras were there when Soviet President Leonid Brezhnev greeted him at the airport, and as the Cuban president was honored with a twenty-one-gun volley of anti-aircraft guns. They filmed as the Cuban entourage was greeted by Muscovites in the Russian capital, and as Dorticós laid a wreath at the tomb of Lenin. The film crews followed him as he visited the Soviet science pavilion and captured pictures of him with the first satellite, and as the rector of Moscow State University awarded him an honorary Doctor of Laws degree. They watched as he visited Leningrad, Volgograd, and Kiev, as he met with young Cubans studying in the Soviet Union—including Fidel's son.

If the Americans weren't steaming yet, Dorticós gave them more to fret over. Instead of flying back to Cuba when he left Moscow, he went to Beijing for a face-to-face meeting with Chairman Mao.

Four days into that trip, he got a chance to address a crowd estimated at one hundred thousand by the Chinese news agency Xinhua and used the chance to poke the United States yet again. He told the cheering crowd that Cuba would kick the United States out of Guantanamo and reclaim the land as its own "through a resolute and tenacious prolonged struggle; the imperialists will have to give up these territories."

Then, with words that surely must have caused more than one case of heartburn in Washington, D.C., and raised an eyebrow or two in Moscow, he added: "Both the Chinese and Cuban peoples are struggling to wipe from the earth the exploitation of man by man. History and destiny have already linked us together and no storm of imperialism can undermine our unity and friendship."

Dorticós came back to Cuba triumphant. He had successfully boosted Cuba's prominence in world politics, irked the United States, and, on his way home, signed a much-needed trade deal with the Soviets and Chinese. The Communist countries had agreed to buy five million tons of sugar a year from Cuba for the next three years. It was a lifesaver for the desperately cash-strapped revolutionary regime in Havana. That was what he was about to announce on the north terrace of the Presidential Palace on that October night.

Some ten thousand people filled the plaza in front of the palace as Dorticós and Castro stepped out to speak. The assassination team in the apartment peered out. All three belonged to counterrevolutionary groups active in the resistance against Castro: Bernardo Paradela, Luis Caicedo, and a man I knew only by his nom de guerre, Freddy.

I wasn't there. I knew that sooner or later, Cuban security forces would trace the attack back to the eighth floor apartment across the street. It would be impossible for my mother-in-law to escape interrogation, or worse. The apartment was undeniably in her name. What she knew, or didn't, could be painfully costly for her. I would never forgive myself if anything happened to her.

The men, I expected, would be OK. They had no link to the apartment, except for me. Inside it, they had all the tools they needed to escape. Along with the bazooka, I had stashed an M1 carbine with three fully loaded ammunition clips, two Czech 9 mm semi-automatic pistols, one of the Tommy guns, five loaded magazines, and five fragmentation grenades. In the closet with the weapons, I also left them their disguises for their escape: three Cuban militia uniforms, with olive green berets, and one rebel army uniform.

They also had two rounds for the bazooka. The crowd was sure to panic as soon as the first hit its target and exploded. To further fuel the mayhem, though, more of our men in the crowd would throw their grenades in different directions. A few random pistol shots would only add to the confusion and send the crowd running wildly in every direction, with no idea where the first blast had come from.

While that pandemonium played out in the plaza, the men in the apartment would slip on the uniforms and make their way down to the street. No one would suspect, or stop, a security official rushing through the bedlam. The men then had designated safe houses where they could discard their uniforms, don civilian clothes, and filter quietly back undercover.

That was the escape plan. For them. But I knew that sooner or later Cuban intelligence would figure out where the bazooka blast had come from. They would find the discarded weapon in the abandoned apartment. And they would come looking for the person who lived there—my mother-in-law. Then they would come looking for me.

So, the night before the planned assassination, after dropping off the bazooka, I had taken my mother-in-law to the coast to meet a waiting boat that would whisk us to safety, and exile, in the United States.

Bishop had urged me to leave. He said things were getting hot. He said he had learned that Castro's intelligence agents suspected me of subversive activity. That coincided with information I had gotten shortly before.

Cuban politics and Cuban families could be—and still are—a complicated tangle of loyalties. One of my cousins, Guillermo Ruiz, held a ranking position in the regime's intelligence agency, the DGI (Dirección General de Inteligencia, in Spanish). He asked to see me one day.

"You were seen," he said when we met. "At the American Embassy."

"Yes?"

"Yes."

It was hard to read his intention. His tone betrayed no emotion. I couldn't tell if I was being offered a warning by my cousin, or if I was about to be arrested by an official with DGI.

"What were you doing there, Antonio?"

"I went to see about visas," I lied, "for friends."

He folded his hands on the desk.

"Really?" he asked.

"Yes," I lied again. "Really."

He studied me for what seemed like a very long moment. Then he unfolded his hands and leaned toward me.

"Then you are using the wrong entrance," he said.

I left thinking that I hadn't really been lying. I had gone to the embassy looking for visas for friends. I just didn't tell my cousin why.

According to a CIA memo uncovered later: "(Deleted) to help in an assassination plot against Castro. Veciana asked for visas for ten relatives of the four men assigned to kill Castro and also requested four M1 rifles with adapters for grenades plus eight grenades. (Deleted) did not encourage Veciana and subsequently checked with (Deleted) who reported that Veciana had made similar 'wild-eyed' proposals to him."

I didn't tell Bishop about the meeting with my cousin. But when he told me he had information that I was being watched, I knew he had very good sources in very good places.

Still, my plan was to put my mother-in-law aboard the boat and go with her to Miami, where I expected my organizational skills would be needed in the ensuing chaos after Castro's demise.

When we got to where the boat was supposed to be waiting, though, we were told that the area was under surveillance. The captain refused to come to the dock. I knew I had to get my mother-in-law off the island, but I didn't know how. She couldn't swim.

I could.

Barely a sliver of moon angled overhead as I pushed her into the water and started swimming, towing her to the boat. I didn't have to tell her to hold on tight. She had no choice. It was slow going, but finally we reached the boat bobbing on the waves in the near dark.

The captain pulled my mother-in-law aboard, then put out his hand to help me out of the water. I hesitated.

"Well?" he asked.

I looked back at the lights on shore, thinking about what was due to occur at the Presidential Palace. This was a historic night, and although I would not be there to pull the trigger, I knew I had served my country, and my people. I had put the pieces in place to give them their freedom, to do with as they chose. Someday soon I hoped to return to Cuba and share it with them.

I took the captain's hand and climbed aboard.

The captain had a small transistor radio. I kept listening as we pulled away from Cuba, as the lights of my homeland disappeared behind me. I listened the next day as we were spotted by a U.S. Coast Guard cutter, and after we were taken aboard for questioning and processing.

I heard nothing. I couldn't understand. I kept asking myself how Castro could have been killed and there could be no word. I kept asking myself what could have happened.

The CIA record says: "October 7, 1961, Veciana entered U.S. at Key West. Had passport, no visa. Came via small boat, received $100 a month refugee assistance."

It didn't mention my involvement in the plot to kill Fidel and Dorticós.

Yet, coincidentally—or not—the same day that the bazooka attack was to occur, President Kennedy's special assistant for national security affairs, McGeorge Bundy, sent a top-secret memorandum to the secretary of state, with copies to Secretary of Defense Robert McNamara, Director of Central Intelligence Allen Dulles, and Richard Goodwin, director of the president's Cuban Task Force. The memo clearly indicates that the Kennedy administration was preparing for Castro's imminent removal from power.

It read:

Washington, October 5, 1961.
SUBJECT: Cuba

In accordance with General [Maxwell] Taylor's instructions, I talked to Assistant Secretary Woodward yesterday about the requirement for the preparation of a contingency plan. He told me on the telephone he would be leaving for two weeks and, therefore, his Deputy, Wymberley Coerr, would have to take this project on.

I then met with Mr. Coerr and outlined the requirement to him. I said that what was wanted was a plan against the contingency that Castro would in some way or other be removed from the Cuban scene. I said that my understanding was the terms of reference governing this plan should be quite broad; we agreed, for example, that the presence and positions of Raul and Che Guevara must be taken into account. We agreed that this was an exercise that should be under the direction of State with participation by Defense and CIA. I also pointed out to Mr. Coerr that Mr. Goodwin had been aware of this requirement.

Mr. Coerr said he would get his people started on this right away. As to timing, I said that I did not understand that this was a crash program but that it should proceed with reasonable speed. He then set Monday as a target date for a first draft.

. . .

On the covert side, I talked to Tracy Barnes in CIA and asked that an up-to-date report be furnished as soon as possible on what is going on and what is being planned.

Barnes was way ahead of him. The very next day, October 6, he sent a memorandum to Jake Esterline, Chief of the Western Hemisphere Division, instructing him to prepare a contingency plan based on the assumption of the unexpected removal of Castro from power. The memo was titled: "What Would Happen If Castro Died?"

The timing was curious, to say the least. Bishop knew fully about the planned assassination attempt with the bazooka. He had to. He had arranged for the apartment to conveniently come available. He had arranged for me to get the weapons I needed. What none of us knew yet was why it had failed.

Much later, after he got out of Cuba and joined me in exile, Bernardo Paradela told me.

The night of the planned attack, the people had filled the square as expected. Castro and Dorticós had stepped out onto the north terrace, as expected. What we had not anticipated, Paradela told me, were the lights.

Whether it was a security measure, or merely an effort at affording dramatic stage lighting for the speech, we may never know. But as darkness fell on the plaza, Castro's technicians turned on giant floodlights, like the searchlights aimed at the sky during the Academy Awards. Instead of aiming them at the sky, though, they shined them on the surrounding buildings and let the bright reflection off the building façades help illuminate the plaza.

One or more of the lights shone directly on the building at No. 29 Avenida de las Misiones where the men with the bazooka waited. The bright light poured through the window into apartment 8-A. Even if they had been able to steady their aim without being spotted, and fired the shot without Castro being pulled to safety first, there was no way they could have escaped. Or so they thought.

I don't know. And I can't say what I would have done if I had been there with them. Others might say they would have taken the chance anyway. Some might have. But I don't know. It's easy to be brave when you're safe in your own home. It's much harder when you have to decide if you're willing to die for a cause.

They decided they weren't.

It didn't matter.

Cuban General Fabián Escalante, who eventually rose to be the head of Cuban intelligence, later said that the government's security forces had learned of the planned attack ahead of time. The night of October 5, he swarmed the area with his men. The hit men in the apartment spooked and fled.

In some versions of the story, the security forces were only minutes behind them. They crashed into the apartment and found the weapons stashed in the closet, along with the uniforms. They had already arrested other members of the resistance, including one they claimed had connections to the CIA and had brought in the plans for the bazooka attack. However it happened, Cuban intelligence quickly uncovered the other weapon stashes. They found the 60 mm mortar and the other Tommy guns, the two light Browning machine guns, and all twenty M1s. And, within days, they captured Paradela and the others.

Maybe I was supposed to leave when I did. Escalante later said they had already identified me as the head of sabotage for the MRP, the People's Revolutionary Movement, and already linked me to David Atlee Phillips and the CIA.

Maybe Escalante was telling the truth. Just days after I arrived in the United States, Cuban intelligence arrested Reynold González, the head of the MRP. I didn't know it when it happened. All I knew was that the attempt to kill Castro had failed.

But I would try again.

chapter 2
AN UNLIKELY TERRORIST

I WAS AN unlikely terrorist. I was skinny, asthmatic, and plagued with insecurities.

The last came as a consequence of the first two, and of my experiences growing up.

I was born on the cusp of the Great Depression. Many think of this as an American event. It wasn't. It was global. As the saying goes, "When America sneezes, the world catches a cold."

This time, America had pneumonia.

A year and a day before I was born, Pan Am made its first international flight, from Key West to Havana. It was symbolic. We had arrived. We were connected through the most modern technology to our neighbor, friend, and benefactor to the north, heralding our heyday.

Eleven days after my first birthday, the New York stock market crashed.

Then, like a tidal wave rushing out from the epicenter of a great tremor, the effects of Black Tuesday thundered around the world. It broke economies and broke people. Cuba, which had prospered magnificently thanks to its privileged relationship with the United States, now crumbled along with it.

The cornerstone of our island economy, the sugar industry, collapsed. Between 1929 and 1932, the price of sugar dropped from roughly two cents a pound to barely half a cent. Together, the "big four"—sugar, tobacco, cigars, and fruit—brought in $363 million to the Cuban economy the year I was born. After the depression hit, prices dropped so much that even though Cuba exported three-fourths as much in goods, it brought in barely one-sixth as much revenue, just $57 million.

The result was a downturn as devastating, or worse, as what happened in the United States. It was, in short, a time of hardship, hunger, and uncertainty. Families lived together because that's what they could afford. Ours was no different. We lived together with my uncles and aunts and cousins—thirteen of us in all—on our little *finquita*. Calling it a farm, even a "little farm," is perhaps a bit too generous. It was a plot of land in what is now one of the most populated neighborhoods in Havana.

My neighborhood was, and is, known as La Víbora. It means "the viper." But there's nothing sinister to the name. Supposedly it comes from the 1700s, when La Víbora was a way station where caravans changed horses on the long trip between Güines and Havana. It was also home to a pharmacy, which identified itself by displaying a medical caduceus, with the twin serpents intertwined. The easy reference to the spot, or so the story goes, was as *la parada de la víbora*, or "the viper stop."

By the time I came along, La Víbora was no longer a separate place from Havana. It kept its uniquely irregular sloping streets and the staircases linking the sidewalks along the thoroughfares, but the one-time highway stop had been absorbed into the capital city much the way New York City swallowed up once-detached areas like the Bronx and Greenwich Village.

My parents were immigrants from Spain who arrived in Cuba at the beginning of the twentieth century. They met on the island and were married. I was their only child. I was ugly and sickly, but I was their world.

My father, a bricklayer, made 6.50 a day. Pesos, not dollars. When he could find work. Often enough, there was none to be found. He might work a couple of weeks, then be off for several more, waiting for the next job. He tried to hide it, but I could feel his anxiety as the desperate, idle days of no work and no income stretched into weeks.

Eating meat in Cuba at that time was a privilege. Still, my parents made sure I ate what they could not afford for themselves, once a week. They didn't. They worried about my health. I was frail, skeletally thin, and seized by recurring bouts of asthma that left me wheezing and fighting for air. There was no medicine to be had. So they did without, and my mother served me meat every week, to strengthen me.

It didn't stop the asthma. The attacks came with frightening and exhausting frequency, leaving me gasping for breath. To alleviate the symptoms, my father would take me down to the Malecón, Havana's famous seawall. We would look out across the moonlight splintering on the waves, and I would suck in the salt air. The sea breeze was the best remedy. My airways opened and my rasping eased as the warm, moist air soothed my inflamed passages.

When I was nine, my life changed. By then, Cuba had already seen its first dictator since gaining its independence, and its first coup. Fulgencio Batista, who would come to be known as the man who lost Cuba to Castro, led the "Revolt of the Sergeants" as I was turning five and held on to power through a series of puppet presidents as Cuba crawled out of the doldrums of the Great Depression. This was all a backdrop to my childhood, to which I, like most children, remained oblivious. I was as ignorant about politics and presidents as I was about the concept of scarcity—in the same way that a fish is unaware that it lives in the sea. It was my world. I knew no other. I played with my cousins and friends and, when I was old enough, went to school. And that is how my life changed.

While my neighborhood friends went to public school, my mother decided she wanted something different for me. The public schools in Havana weren't very good. But La Víbora was home to one of the most respected private institutions on the island. The Colegio Champagnat–Hermanos Maristas was part of the worldwide network of schools established and operated by the Catholic order of Marist Brothers. Ours, like many, was named after the order's founder, St.

Marcellin Champagnat, and provided schooling from pre-school to pre-university.

It also provided—and demanded—religious training in the Catholic tradition. That meant going to mass every day, from 8:00 to 8:30 a.m., followed by a half hour of catechism.

The school was exceptional, but it was also private, and, to my family's humble means, expensive. My mother, however, would not be dissuaded. She went after the school's administrators with the same single-minded determination that would mark me. The school wanted six pesos a month for tuition. My mother argued for three months until they finally agreed, perhaps just to be free of her, to reduce it to four.

And so, starting in the third grade, I began a life of discipline that would mark me forever.

When Castro took over, the Communists closed the school. They looted its contents and took the teachers' personal property. They stripped away the religious trappings and turned the school into a training ground for the "new men and women" of the Revolution.

It remained, however, a massive and stately building, with great Doric columns framing the entrance and lining the wings surrounding the grand center courtyard. It was, to me, a majestic place, a true institution of learning and faith, standing regally on a steeply slanting road overlooking the city stretching out below. It was a place that seemed to demand respect, and that is what I gave it.

Every morning, as I said, we gathered in the large and imposing chapel for morning mass. It stretched past rows and rows of dark pews to the altar and its ornately decorated apse with a life-sized Christ on a crucifix rising above it all. As I sat pressed in among the other students, the reverberating thrum of the priest's voice seemed like heaven's thunder, inspiring awe and obedience.

The brothers taught us the practice of "the treasure." Every week we wrote down the sacrifices that we had made during the days before. I would only eat half of my desert, or not go out at playtime. It taught me discipline. Every week, I wanted to be the one deemed "the most religious." Nearly every week, I was. And later, when I was older, I was the only Marist selected as one of the directors of the National

Federation of Cuban Catholic Youth. It was, as its name implied, a union of young faithful, calling on us to partake in a life of intense spirituality, prayer, and retreats. I'm sure it's only a coincidence that it was founded the year of my birth, with a motto that might have been my own: "Faith, Study, and Action."

Still, it seems appropriate to note here that later in my life, after Castro came to power, I lost my faith—not in God, but in religion. I stayed home and meditated, practicing my faith that way. But I stopped believing in religion.

While I was in school, though, I took pride in being more religious than my schoolmates. I found pleasure in adhering to the rules and rigid order imposed by the brothers.

I fit right in. I was a timid youth, incapable of overstepping the bounds adults set for me. I was more inclined to sacrifice diversion for my studies or work. I loved sports, but my asthma prevented me from participating. So I poured myself into my schooling, striving continually to be not only the favorite among the brothers because of my dedication to religion, but also to be the best among my peers academically. Especially in math. I discovered I had a talent for numbers and a knack for organization. Together, those skills served me well. They led me to a career in accounting and management and, in what was then a completely unforeseen fashion, in my anti-Castro efforts.

Despite that, I felt that my classmates looked down on me. They called me a laborer's son—effectively, a commoner, someone less worthy who had somehow managed to slip past the guards and into a classroom where he didn't belong.

I later realized that the combination of the asthma that kept me from joining in any strenuous physical activities with the other boys, the sense that I was viewed as not being good enough, and the strict demands of my school gave me an inferiority complex that pursued me into adulthood.

My constant struggle with illness, though, ended up strengthening me. My unbreakable will came as the result of that long and sometimes agonizing fight to achieve health. It taught me I should never say never. Especially when, at seventeen, my asthma miraculously disappeared.

Shortly after, I graduated from the Marist school and enrolled in the school of business at the University of Havana. The university had a long history of strident student political activity, and political violence. Students had risen up in rebellion against President Gerardo Machado and his repressive government. Rival political gangs regularly carried guns and didn't hesitate to use them. While I was there, it was no different. And while I was there, so was Fidel. He studied law. I studied accounting. I knew him, but we moved in different circles. He was very aggressive, with strong political aims, even then, and he always surrounded himself with people who were prone to violence.

I did not. I studied. And I fell in love. We met at a party. I was twenty. She wasn't yet fifteen, but she looked twenty. Not just her body, but her face, and her demeanor.

The party was at her cousin's house. The instant I saw her, I was taken with her. I was afraid to speak to her, but I did. Her name, she told me, was Sira. She had been born in Sitges, Spain, a beach town near Barcelona. Her father had died, and her mother had brought her and her sister to Cuba. They had been there less than five years when we met.

After that, we started to go out. In 1953, she became my wife. We had five children and stayed together for nearly fifty years, until she died in 2002. She was an exceptional wife and a sensational mother. I knew she would be even before I married her.

I had taken a position as an accountant with the architectural firm of Arrellano and Batista while Sira and I were dating. I was still studying at the university when I started, dividing my time between my classes at the university's campus in the Vedado district and the firm's office across town, near the famed Bodeguita del Medio restaurant. She never complained about the long hours I spent away from her. Not then, nor later, when the hours I neglected her grew even longer, while I was preparing for a position at the National Bank. Nor later, when my anti-Castro work would take me away from her for days or even weeks at a time.

We were betrothed but not yet married when I graduated from the university and left the architects' office to take a job at the relatively new Banco de Fomento Agrícola e Industrial de Cuba, the Agricultural and Industrial Development Bank. It meant a promotion and a jump in salary of more than a third over what I was making.

BANFAIC's purpose was simple. Cuba, at that point, existed largely as a sugar economy. BANFAIC was created to facilitate credit to non-sugar agriculture and industries and, thereby, to stimulate economic diversity and expansion. Rural credit associations in various parts of the island served as the bank's affiliates, offering low-cost credit for a wide range of endeavors.

When Batista took over in 1952, he saw its potential immediately. At the time, BANFAIC was a little over a year old. It held a portfolio of approximately $720,000 in outstanding loans. In the year that I was there, that amount exploded, to $5 million.

The impact of the increased activity soon became obvious. The total area of land planted with rice nearly doubled, and output shot up over 150 percent. Potatoes, dairy products, beans, tomatoes, and other food commodities also received assistance.

It wasn't just a farm assistance plan, by any means. With an eye on increasing tourism (and, surely, currying favor with Batista's casino-running mobster friends), funds went to developing hotels. Among the projects, for example, was the remodeling of the jewel of Havana's accommodations, the Hotel Nacional.

Batista had political aims, naturally. He wanted to win over the populace, and what better way to gain the support of a poor and hungry people than by increasing food production and creating jobs?

But all was not well under Batista. Corruption and graft kept much of the population in abject poverty. Horrible slums—row upon row of decrepit shanties thrown together from whatever scraps their owners could cobble together—swelled within sight of the very same opulent hotels and casinos that were supposed to boost the economy and improve living conditions.

When Sira and I first married, Batista had returned to the presidency. He had been elected once before, in 1940, and peacefully relinquished the reins of power when his term ended. In 1952, he ran again. When it was clear that he was going to lose, some three months before the election, he staged a coup d'état, ousting then-President Carlos Prío Socarrás, and took the presidency by force.

The repression grew from there. So did the resistance. Me included.

I had graduated with my CPA and started work when Batista seized power. But I have a bit of a rebellious spirit in me. His blatant disregard for our country's Constitution and the rule of democracy inspired me. I, like so many others of my generation, became involved in the resistance movements against Batista.

Fidel took up arms. But he needed money to buy food and weapons and bullets. That is how I could help. I founded a magazine for accountants and worked with the professional groups to sell bonds to raise money for the anti-Batista fighters. With the help of other bank employees, we funneled money under the noses of the government's overseers to finance the Second National Front of Escambray. The rebels attacked from their mountain strongholds. I worked against Batista from within the system, lending both clandestine and, on at least one very public occasion, overt support.

That incident came, indirectly perhaps, as a result of Castro—because of the rebel attack he led against Batista's army at the Moncada Barracks in Santiago.

Sira and I were married May 15, 1953. My best man was Boris Luis Santa Coloma. Two months later, he was dead.

Boris and I were born just weeks apart but didn't meet until we enrolled at the University of Havana. Both of us majored in business or, as it was called in the school at the time, commercial sciences. We became fast friends, and so when the time came, it seemed only natural that it would be he whom I would ask to stand as my groomsman as I took Sira's hand in marriage. I knew Boris was a man of honor, and I was honored to have him by my side.

I also knew he was vocally opposed to Batista. He was active in the student movement aimed at ousting Batista, and on July 26, he joined with Fidel in the attack on Moncada. It began at 6 a.m. and quickly turned into a disaster. When it became obvious that the assault had failed, Castro ordered the 135 or so rebel fighters to retreat.

From what we were told afterward, Boris went into the hospital behind the barracks to search out other members of the rebel force who had been sent to take it. He never made it back. He was captured, tortured, and killed. Photographs released afterward showed his shirtless, bullet-riddled body lying on a tile floor. His boyish face, with the thin wisp of mustache he had grown before the wedding, was smeared with blood. He was twenty-four.

I was stunned, and angry. I seethed for a year, as things worsened in Cuba. On the anniversary of his death, I organized a memorial service in Boris's honor at the university. I knew the risk. Batista's police were thugs and assassins who wouldn't hesitate to kill someone they saw as an enemy—or anyone else for that matter. And Batista unleashed them against whomever he pleased.

Standing up publicly to pay my respects to someone who had been involved in the first armed uprising against Batista would surely be seen as opposition to him. It had the very real potential of marking me as an enemy of the government. And that, in Batista's Cuba, could surely bring repercussions. Possibly lethal ones.

I didn't care. One of my core personality traits is a strong sense of loyalty and responsibility. So, on July 26, 1954, I stood before a group of Boris's friends, students, activists, and, I'm sure, Batista's undercover watchdogs and said that I was proud to have known him, and proud of him.

Curiously, for reasons that remain a mystery to me, nothing happened. No one threatened me. No one even came to question me. In fact, despite the fears others close to me surely felt, I continued without any difficulties at my job in the most important government bank on the island.

The year of the Moncada assault was my last year with BANFAIC. I spent six months studying and preparing myself to be accepted for a position at the Banco Nacional—in effect, Cuba's Federal Reserve. Sira again proved herself to be the ideal wife and partner. We were newly married, but she never complained as I filled all my waking moments outside of my full-time work by burying myself in books and study.

I can never repay her devotion, nor the time I stole from our new marriage, but some small reward came at the end of that half-year. I was accepted as a bank inspector at the Banco Nacional as 1953 came to a close. I was twenty-five years old. It was a prestigious position, especially for someone so young, and it brought a hefty increase in salary. Our income shot from three hundred pesos per month to five hundred.

That same year also saw a massive surge in Batista's oppression, and in the opposition to him. After Moncada, more organizations joined with what was now known as the July 26 Movement. It was no longer just students, political opponents, and the disenfranchised. Now support involved people from all walks of life—lawyers, doctors, and, like me, accountants.

It was a long, frustrating, and bloody fight. Batista responded to the opposition against him with increasing brutality. He suspended constitutional protections and strengthened the oppressive apparatus. Eventually, he closed the university and turned the country into a police state. Young men my age were tortured and publicly executed, left hanging from lampposts throughout the city as a warning to others.

In an often-quoted John F. Kennedy speech, made twelve days before my thirty-second birthday and while he was still a young senator campaigning for the White House, Kennedy put the number murdered by Batista's forces at twenty thousand in the seven years of his stolen presidency.

It was, the young senator noted, "a greater proportion of the Cuban population than the proportion of Americans who died in both World Wars." Batista, Kennedy continued, "turned democratic Cuba into a complete police state—destroying every individual liberty. . . . Yet, our aid to his regime, and the ineptness of our policies, enabled Batista to invoke the name of the United States in support of his reign of terror."

They were dark days for Cuba. And it was hardly limited to Havana. The oppression spread across the island, in cities and villages alike. As the opposition grew, Batista's brutality escalated. "His men were out to stamp out opposition and end a revolution," the Associated Press reported. "Civil rights meant nothing in Cuba . . ."

The number of deaths attributed to members of Batista's regime was staggering, and hardly restricted to Havana alone. "One man alone, Maj. Jesus Sosa Blanco, was accused of responsibility for 108 victims," according to the AP. Witnesses later testified that five of Sosa's soldiers executed nineteen villagers suspected of supporting Castro's rebels, including nine members of a single family lined up and machine-gunned together.

A priest sent out to search for four university students tortured and hanged just four days before Batista abandoned the island said he found their bodies "heaped in a mound and covered by about four inches of dirt." During the search, he said, he discovered other mounds "containing groups of 30, 50 and 80, all victims apparently of the inhuman repression at Pinar del Rio . . ."

Castro, and the July 26 Movement, only grew stronger. They burned sugar cane fields, destroyed mills. They attacked the Belot oil refinery and even, once, entered the Banco Nacional and took a group of employees hostage. I was no longer with the bank when it happened. The rebels didn't hurt anyone, but they set a fire and burned the previous day's checks and bank drafts.

Despite having American-supplied planes and weapons, Batista's military showed itself to be dismally ineffective against the rebels in the Sierra Maestra and Escambray. By the end of 1958, the "Bearded Ones," as the scruffy revolutionaries came to be known, had defeated Batista's military in a series of battles and were advancing steadily through Santa Clara province, west of Havana.

The reign of terror ended January 1, 1959. Batista fled the country.

We soon learned the truth behind the old saying: "Better the devil you know than the devil you don't."

chapter 3
THE BEARDED ONES

WHEN FIDEL CASTRO came to power in Cuba on January 1, 1959, David Atlee Phillips was already there.

In fact, the man who just months later would introduce himself to me as Maurice Bishop takes credit as "the first American intelligence source in Cuba to report the departure of Batista." In the somewhat fanciful memoir Phillips penned of his CIA exploits after retirement, *The Night Watch*, he wrote:

Helen [his wife at the time] and I had been at a New Year's Eve party, bidding *adios* to 1958, and, returning home, we had a final glass of champagne while relaxing in lawn chairs outside. A large airplane flew over the house about 4 a.m. I telephoned my case officer.

"Batista just flew into exile," I said.

"Are you drunk?" he asked.

"Feeling okay," I admitted. "But I know there are no scheduled air flights in Cuba at four in the morning. And a commercial airliner just took off and headed out over the ocean. If Batista is not aboard I'll eat your sombrero."

Bishop was right, of course, and when Fidel Castro marched into Havana seven days later, he claimed to be among the crowds welcoming the conquering hero. He might've been glad to see Batista's brutality at an end, but he had other, more personal, reasons as well. After serving briefly in a CIA posting in the Cuban capital a few years earlier, the man I knew as Bishop had recently resigned from the agency and returned to the island as a private businessman, with a plan.

David Atlee Phillips had a colorful background. A World War II vet with a smooth radio announcer's voice and dreams of acting, Phillips had taken the earnings from a play he wrote about his experiences in a German prisoner-of-war camp and moved his young family to Chile in 1948. He bought an English-language newspaper and some printing equipment. That caught the attention of the local CIA station chief, and, two years after his arrival in Santiago, Phillips began his career with the agency as a part-time operative.

Over the following decade, he went on to serve in Washington, D.C., Guatemala, Havana, and Beirut. In late 1958, he became convinced that Fidel Castro would win and Batista would be deposed. The change in government, he felt, would create a need for a Spanish-speaking American public relations firm that could act as a bridge to smooth connections with the incoming administration.

So, according to his account of events, Phillips resigned from the CIA, relocated his family back to Havana, and established his new business, David A. Phillips Associates. He might have resigned officially, but he didn't quit entirely. In his own words, he offered to help the CIA's Havana chief of station in a part-time capacity. And that is how we came to meet.

I had left the Banco Nacional before Fidel declared victory. I went to work for Julio Lobo, the richest man in Cuba. Lobo was Cuba's first millionaire and, at the time of the revolution, its richest man. His personal fortune was so immense, people in Havana and Miami still wistfully exclaim, "To be as rich as Julio Lobo!"

Born in Venezuela, Lobo was, in his time, considered to be the most powerful sugar broker in the world. He was much more than that. In 1959, his holdings reportedly included fourteen sugar mills— six he owned outright; he held the controlling interest in eight more— and more than three hundred thousand acres of surrounding sugar cane fields and land. In addition, he owned 23 percent of the shares in the giant U.S.-owned West Indies Sugar Corp., twenty sugar warehouses, an insurance company, a telegraph and telephone company, a shipping line with four subsidiaries, an oil company, three refineries, and an airline.

He also owned, as the writer John Paul Rathbone noted in *The Sugar King of Havana*, "the largest collection of Napoleonic memorabilia outside France." It included, among other things, the emperor's death mask and one of his teeth. His personal art collection included works by Leonardo da Vinci, Raphael, Michelangelo, Goya, Diego Rivera, and Salvador Dalí.

And he owned a bank, the Banco Financiero, with more than $12 million in deposits, thirteen branches, and eighty-six employees— including, beginning in 1958, me. I was his vice president and comptroller. I worked in the bank's main building, a stunning colonial classic of solid stone block standing formidably on a corner of Obispo Street, in the heart of Old Havana.

Lobo paid me what was then the lofty sum of seven hundred and fifty pesos a month—a full 50 percent more than my previous job at the Banco Nacional had paid. It was a lot to me, but surely nothing to Cuba's so-called "Sugar King," estimated to be worth more than $200 million. Then. That would equal more than $5 billion today.

The Banco Financiero was exactly what its name suggested: a finance bank, a lending bank that helped fund the great expansion of private investment in Cuba during the 1950s. Those were heady days in Havana. Tourism was booming. The island became the destination of choice for Americans looking for a sunny, exotic getaway that was closer than Las Vegas was from the Eastern seaboard cities, with their gloomy wintertimes.

Havana first gained its notoriety as a playground for the rich in the Roaring Twenties, but the prosperous years after World War II brought a new rush of entertainment-hungry tourists from the American middle class. It was cheap, warm, and welcoming, with unfettered gambling and liberal laws. American investors, too, took notice. The history books give the most attention to mobsters like Meyer Lansky, Lucky Luciano, and Santo Trafficante, Jr., but the mafia bosses were hardly the only ones to seek development opportunities in Cuba.

By the time I went to work at the Banco Financiero, "U.S. financial interests included 90 percent of Cuban mines, 80 percent of its public utilities, 50 percent of its railways, 40 percent of its sugar production and 25 percent of its bank deposits—some $1 billion in total," according to *Smithsonian* magazine.

Hoteliers such as John McEntee Bowman, who bought the Hotel Sevilla-Biltmore, had led the way decades before. By the end of the 1950s, though, the lure of gargantuan casino profits under Batista's contentedly corrupt regime brought a building boom, and Lobo was far too shrewd a businessman to be left on the sidelines. The Banco Financiero played a part in funding the construction of Hollywood actor George Raft's Hotel Capri and Casino, with its famous rooftop pool nineteen stories in the sky above Havana, and Meyer Lansky's twenty-one-story, 440-room Hotel Riviera overlooking the seafront Malecón. Designed and built in just six months by one of the founders of the Miami Modern architectural style, the Riviera cost $8 million— nearly $70 million today.

Those were the boom times, when even such an extravagant sum seemed paltry compared to the riches to be reaped over the years to come.

"We close only for revolutions," José Orozco García, manager of the notorious nightclub Shanghai Theater, told *Cabaret* magazine writer Jay Mallin in 1956. "We aren't bothered by anything else."

He couldn't have been more prescient.

On the day of Batista's departure, the casinos were smashed and looted. According to Herbert Matthews, the *New York Times* reporter who famously met with Fidel and the rebels in the Sierra Maestra early on in the fight, a mob of looters first attacked the Sevilla Biltmore. "Rightly or wrongly, the casinos and slot machines are connected in the public mind with gangsters, police protection and the corruption of the Batista regime and they have also been condemned by Fidel Castro's rebel movement," he wrote. A couple of paragraphs later, he continued: "A mob burst into the lobby of the Sevilla Biltmore Hotel and started breaking things up. Then it went outside and began smashing every shop window along the street called Calle Trocadero."

They smashed some windows at the Hotel Capri, Matthews reported, and a photo accompanying the piece showed a policeman aiming his rifle at two men coming out of the Hotel Plaza, where, the caption said, "a gambling casino was wrecked following flight of Fulgencio Batista."

I did not read the *New York Times* article the following morning, but the news of what had happened raced through the streets of the capital. I was not surprised. Matthews was right. The casinos served as a symbol of Batista's brutal rule for a people who had suffered so much for so long. Now, with the strongman gone, they vented their ire on the businesses connected to his associates.

And Castro took almost no time to satisfy their hunger for revenge. Exactly two weeks after arriving in Havana, he closed the casinos. Permanently.

I had always doubted Fidel, ever since I met him. But in the first glow of the Revolution, nearly everyone saw him as a hero. Even members of my family. I have a daughter who was born in April 1959. The family gave her the name Zoila Victoria. Sounded out, it was, "*Soy La Victoria*"—"I am the Victory."

To me, though, Castro seemed to be just a variation of Batista—someone who seized power under the pretense of doing it for the people but who, in the end, only wanted power for himself. Some say Fidel led the assault on Moncada because Batista halted the 1952 election. Castro, then a young lawyer, had been nominated to run as an Ortodoxo Party candidate to Cuba's House of Representatives. Shutting down the election killed his chance.

Fidel Castro and I were of the same generation. We were in different disciplines at the University of Havana, but I got to know him well. He was one of the student gangsters, a member of the Unión Insurreccional Revolucionaria that was battling for control of the university, and supported violence as a means to that end. One of the directors of the UIR later confessed to me that Fidel participated in various assaults that ended in the death of his student adversaries. The authorities accused him on two different occasions of having participated in the assassination of university leaders. Once he attained power, he cut loose his friends and gangster companions, facilitating their travels outside of the country.

The whole time he lived in Havana, he lived off the money his father sent him and whatever money he could obtain through extortions. He grew accustomed to living without working. He was always distant from his family. He got his education haphazardly in a climate of tension where the strongest bullied and eliminated competitors. At the time, Fidel had more of a Fascist inclination than a Communist one, but his lust for power was obvious. I remained wary.

The CIA had been suspicious of him for just as long. In the agency's "Official History of the Bay of Pigs Operation," CIA historian Jack Pfeiffer wrote: "Fidel CASTRO RUZ was identified in one of the earliest reports in Agency files as 'one of the young, student leaders in Cuba, who manages to get himself involved in many things that do not concern him.'"

A decade later, Castro was a force to be reckoned with and a growing preoccupation for the CIA. According to Pfeiffer, agency officials primarily wanted to know, "Is he, or is he not, a Communist?"

It was enough of a worry, wrote Pfeiffer, that the CIA infiltrated Castro's rebel forces in the mountains in order to spy on him: "By early 1958, the Agency had become sufficiently concerned about the pro-communist orientation of Castro's government, and particularly the pro-Castro proclivities of his two principal deputies, Ernesto Che Guevara and Raúl Castro Ruz, Fidel's brother, that penetration of the Partido Socialista Popular was a priority concern of the field. At least two agents were successfully placed in PSP ranks, and in March 1958, one Agency officer managed to join the Castro forces in the mountains for a period of two weeks and to observe their tactics in combat."

Castro, however, kept his true colors hidden—and the CIA guessing. It was only in the days just before Fidel took over, President Dwight Eisenhower later wrote, that the head of the agency, Allen Dulles, told him for the first time that "Communists and other extreme radicals appear to have penetrated the Castro government. If Castro takes over, they will probably participate in the government."

Still, it took many in Cuba by surprise when it happened.

My generation was the one that came to power with the revolution. I had been part of the civic institutions that were opposed to Batista. I had friends who were in the new revolutionary government. The minister of finance, Rufo López Fresquet, was a friend of mine. He invited me to leave my job with Julio Lobo and join the government. I considered it. But when I told my wife, she said, "Don't even think about that."

Government workers in Cuba had always had a bad reputation. Not just the ones in Batista's administration. There was always corruption. So the people associated with the government were not well regarded. By 1959, I had arrived at a prestigious position in a private institution. Sira was right. It would be crazy for me to leave the bank and join the government because of some idealism.

So I stayed at the Banco Financiero. But I had relations with people in the government, and shortly after Fidel and the rebels took control of the government, party leaders in the July 26 Movement called me. I had been editor of the Professional Accountants' Association's magazine. They wanted me to run for head of the association again, as a candidate of the July 26 Movement.

National politics had never played a part in the professional associations. I told them that, and I explained to them that I did not aspire to anything. They insisted. They said I had to be part of the July 26 Movement's slate of candidates. The pressure was so great that they made me go see the finance minister and the president of the court of accounts so that they could convince me. I said no. But they pushed so hard that it made me angry. I decided that I would stand up to them. I decided to run as the candidate of the party opposing the July 26 Movement.

That created a difficult situation for me with the government.

Worse, when the elections happened, I thought I would lose. I didn't. I won. Overwhelmingly. I don't think the people voted for me; they voted against them.

The government reacted by taking over the accountants' association. They made it and its members part of July 26 Movement anyway, as if that's what we had been all along.

I prepared a circular denouncing the takeover. Back then, what we had were mimeograph machines. I wrote that it was unjust for them to take over the association, that we had done nothing but to act in the interest of the professional accountants. I never got to send out my leaflet.

Someone with the bank employees union got his hands on it. He gave it to Cuban intelligence, G2. I was in a meeting at the bank when one of their sergeants came to arrest me. He took me back to his headquarters to see a lieutenant there. The lieutenant went on to be the number three man in Cuba. His name was Carlos Aldana.

He treated me very well.

"What's happening?" he asked me. "Why are you going against the revolution?"

I said, "*Oye*, Lieutenant, I'm not going against the revolution. I merely have the interest of my professional organization in mind. That flyer is not a secret. That flyer is public. I'm going to send it to everyone."

We talked for a while longer.

"Are you married?" he asked. "Do you have kids?"

I told him I was, and that we had three.

"You don't need to be in politics," he said.

And he let me go.

THE GOVERNMENT HAD not taken over the bank yet, and I kept on working as its comptroller. Lobo wasn't political. His party was money. When others started leaving Cuba, he stayed. He had no choice. He had built up many debts outside of the country to buy assets in Cuba, so he couldn't leave the country. All of his wealth was in Cuba. If he came to the United States, he would find himself buried in debt. He'd be ruined. Plus, I think he honestly believed Fidel wouldn't last.

Journalist William Attwood later said that when he traveled to Cuba for *Look* magazine in July 1959, "I was told quite flatly by Julio

Lobo . . . that Castro would not live out the year, there was a contract on him." Attwood, who later served as a diplomat in the Kennedy administration, went on to tell the Church Committee in the 1970s that "assassination was in the air" during his trip to Cuba after Castro's victory. At a party where he saw some CIA officers, he testified, guests talked "quite openly about assassinating Castro."

That same month, Cuba's president, Manuel Urrutia, resigned over concerns about Communist influence in the government. By the end of the year, Castro's Communist leanings were increasingly apparent, and more of his ministers quit or were ousted. Huber Matos, Castro's military leader in Camagüey, resigned in October. He was arrested the following day, charged with treason, and sentenced to twenty years in prison.

What I had suspected all along was coming true. Fidel burned with desire for political power. He achieved it in the bloom of youth. And once achieved, he longed to enjoy it until the last day of his existence. In order to perpetuate his hold on power indefinitely, he fathered a Communist revolution in Cuba. He applied terror, mercilessly ordering death or prison for his opponents. The abuses, insults, and tortures those political prisoners suffered was only part of their horrible sentence. The worst punishment was to rob them of the best years of life.

Unbeknownst to me, another part of this story was playing out in Havana that summer. It was a distant and tangential incident, but it involved someone whose role in history would intersect with mine later, and with Kennedy's assassination. Jack Ruby, whom the world would come to know as the man who killed Lee Harvey Oswald, was visiting Cuba in the summer of 1959. Cuban immigration records showed Ruby "entered Cuba from New Orleans on August 8, 1959, and left on September 11, 1959."

This was a hot time for Ruby's associates in Havana's criminal underworld. Castro had done more than just close the casinos. He wanted to rid the island of the mob bosses who ran them. In June, he ordered the arrest of all foreign citizens connected to the gambling industry. One of them was Santo Trafficante, Jr., the Tampa mobster who ran the Sans Souci and was widely believed to manage all the syndicate-owned casinos in Havana. After the Kennedy assassination, a British journalist named John Wilson Hudson called the U.S. Embassy in London to report that he had been jailed in Cuba in the summer of 1959. While behind bars, Hudson told embassy officials, "an American gangster called Santo [had been] visited by an American gangster type named Ruby."

CURIOUSLY, ALTHOUGH PROBABLY only coincidentally, David Phillips came to meet me for the first time just a few days after Jack Ruby departed Cuba. I was in my office at the bank, on the top floor, when I got a call from the receptionist. "There's a gentleman here to see you," she said. "A Mr. Maurice Bishop. He wants to speak with you."

The name meant nothing to me.

"All right," I said. "Send him up."

He wore a gray suit with a tie. I would later come to know that he always dressed sharply. His hair was always neatly trimmed and perfectly combed. He had rugged good looks, an actor's face, and a salesman's smooth grace. He spoke perfect Spanish, but with an American accent.

"How may I serve you?" I asked.

He handed me a business card. I don't remember the company's name, but I know it was Belgian. Some sort of mining firm.

He told me he wished to speak with me about a very important matter that required strict confidentiality.

"Is this a business or personal matter?" I asked.

"I want to explain who I am and why I'm here."

His answer made him seem mysterious. It piqued my interest. That may have been his intention. I waited for him to go on.

"I know that you can be trusted," he continued. "I've reviewed our file on you in detail."

"File?"

"About your life," he said. "Who you are. Some of the ideas you've expressed."

My curiosity overwhelmed me. Who was this man? What did he know about me? And why?

For the span of an hour, Bishop provided a detailed account of my life story. He knew the people in my circle of friends, about my family, about my professional triumphs, my political ideas, and my feelings of opposition to the revolutionary government. On this last topic, he seemed to be extraordinarily well informed.

"Where did you get all this information?" I demanded.

He merely smiled.

"And I still don't know who you are, or why you've come to see me," I continued. "You know a lot about me, and what I think. I'm guessing you're with the United States government. Am I right?"

He answered unequivocally.

"I'm not here as a representative of the United States government," he said, "but I am here on behalf of a U.S. intelligence agency."

Perhaps he learned to be so direct from the agent who recruited him in Chile. I was taken aback.

"What do you want with me?" I asked.

"Cuba is going through challenging times," he said. "Dangerous times. It's important for intelligent and determined people to be willing to help prevent it from continuing on its current path."

He paused, looking me directly in the eyes. Then he smiled again, warmly this time.

"If you'd be willing to listen to a proposition, I'd like to invite you to lunch," he said. "So that we can continue our conversation."

I couldn't just then, but we agreed to meet for lunch the next day at 1 p.m. at the famous Floridita. The iconic bar and restaurant was just a few blocks from the bank, a short walk along old Havana's crowded principal path, Obispo Street.

The Floridita claimed it was the birthplace of the daiquiri. Whether or not that was true, it was definitely true that the famed author Ernest Hemingway could be found there regularly downing one after another of the frozen drinks. In his book, Phillips claims he saw the writer there once.

It was my drink of choice, too, anytime I went to the Floridita. This time would be no different.

Bishop was already there when I arrived, although it took me a few moments to pick him out, as I stepped out of the blazing midday sun and into the bar's dark interior.

Once my eyes adjusted to the dim light inside, I spotted him at the bar, nursing a martini. He greeted me warmly and asked the bartender to get me a drink. I ordered my daiquiri and took it with me as a waiter led us to a table.

We had barely looked at the menu and ordered when Bishop began. Again, he was remarkably direct.

"I," he said, "or rather we, are concerned about the direction Cuba is taking. You are, too."

I nodded.

"Yes," he continued. "I know. That is why I have come to you and expect that you will accept my proposal to help us in our efforts."

"Mr. Bishop," I said, "it is true that I am very concerned about the authoritarian path that Fidel Castro's government is taking, but surely you must understand that I can't respond to a proposition without knowing the details."

"Of course. But not here. Not now. These are difficult times." He glanced around the bar quickly, now nearly full with lunchtime patrons. "Dangerous times."

Some might have regarded Bishop/Phillips as unnecessarily fearful. Castro's regime had not yet cranked up the repressive machinery for which it would become famous later. We did not yet have to worry about the constant vigilance of the government's network of eyes and ears, the ready betrayals, or the climate of fear. That would come. Fidel would prove himself an eager student of the KGB's tactics. But it was still early.

Still, the signs were there. The *actos de repudio*, the ugly, "spontaneous" assaults on "antigovernment" individuals and those perceived to be "enemies of the state," had begun. Vicious mobs surrounded whoever it was. They screamed insults, shook their fists angrily, and frequently threw garbage or human feces at the accused. People lost their jobs for grumbling about the government, or just because someone said they did.

Also, the executions that had begun with former police, military officers, and government officials accused of brutality, torture, and murder against the populace now continued with others accused of various forms of treason. As the dozens of executions became hundreds, and the enemies from the previous government were eliminated, the regime turned to enemies of the new. They got summary trials and then were lined up to face the firing squads.

Others, like Matos, found themselves behind bars, serving out sentences in dank and dingy cells, rarely, if ever, allowed visitors. They remained like living ghosts, haunting reminders of what can come to pass for those the government felt threatened by—disappeared, in plain view.

The truth is, Castro had charisma. But he was also taking measures.

So, while the repression was nowhere near the level it would get to, where nearly everyone on the island lived in fear, it paid to be cautious. Bishop continued, in general terms.

"Communism is a bad thing. The Communist elements in the government are gaining influence. Castro hinted at it at the May Day rally. President Urrutia complained about it when he resigned in July. Whether they name it as the reason or not, more high-ranking officials, ministers, are resigning or being removed."

He was right, of course. Intelligent, educated men who had flocked to Fidel's side in his government's opening days were now denouncing it, in word or in deed, showing their disaffection by stepping down.

I had always been an open book about my feelings about Fidel. Even with his finance minister, my friend Rufo López Fresquet, the one who offered me a government position. When I turned him down, I said, "This guy reminds me of Porfirio Díaz, who switched from being a revolutionary to being a dictator."

"Castro?" Rufo responded. "You're wrong. I know him. We are in the presence of a man who has the intellectual level of Martí, Maceo, and Máximo Gómez."

I was surprised, to say the least. Here was someone I would consider an intellectual, someone I knew, a man highly regarded for his knowledge, education, and acumen, one of Cuba's leading voices on matters of finance and the national economy—even before accepting the post as minister—comparing Castro to some of Cuba's greatest minds, our fathers of independence.

He was my friend, so I doubt he ever mentioned my comments to anyone else. And I didn't argue with him. But I know, in the end, he ended up agreeing with me. It hadn't happened yet, at the time of my meeting with Bishop, but in just a handful of months, Rufo López would be out, too. And when I saw him then, he was terrified, wondering what the government might do to him next.

Now, though, Bishop seemed to be able to see the future.

"There will be more," he said. "Things will get worse."

He looked at me steadily before continuing.

"Things will get worse unless capable people, people like you, prevent it from happening. You can help us organize a resistance against Castro's government. It would be a matter of time and intelligent labor. I believe you can do it."

He paused, locking my eyes again. "Are you willing to cooperate?"

"But cooperate with what?" My voice dropped to a whisper. "Are you with the CIA?"

He left the question hanging as took a bite of his food, chewed, and swallowed. I didn't realize it then, but he was working his magic on me. His air of mystery, his confidence, the sense of joining some grand conspiracy—for good—were all seductively appealing. So was his directness.

"I'm with an intelligence service. Don't worry about which one. Are you willing to cooperate?"

I was stunned. I stammered something about it being too soon, too hard to agree without knowing the details of what I was being asked to do.

"I assure you that it's not too soon," he said. "The time has come to act. Your time."

I never thought of being of politician in Cuba. And I certainly didn't think of being a spy. Not even of being a counterrevolutionary. I thought of being a professional, perhaps getting to an important position. I was an accountant, for God's sake. I was surprised that they would be interested in me, that they would believe in me—an American intelligence service!

Looking back, I think I had a double personality I didn't realize I had. But they did. Because later, the things I did in Cuba . . . I would never have imagined on my own. Not without Bishop. He brought out a spirit of adventure I didn't know I had.

"Yes," I said. "I'll do it."

chapter 4
A CONSPIRATOR'S COMMANDMENTS

BISHOP SMILED.

My answer was what he had been hoping for and, I believe as I look back now, expecting. He had led me to a place I didn't know existed, and uncovered a part of me that was foreign.

"Good," he said. "I had hoped so."

I glanced around, trying not to look as apprehensive as I felt. "What do we do now?" I asked.

"Now?" he responded. He leaned in, conspiratorially. "Now we finish our lunch." He raised his glass, signaling the waiter for another. "Then I'll be in touch," he added. "There are certain tests you'll need to go through before we go further."

"Tests? Like a written test? Or a physical examination?"

He chuckled.

"No," he said. "Although we will be checking your pulse."

He smiled at my confusion. "We need to ask some questions," he explained, "quite a few, as a matter of fact. To know more about you. About what you think."

"But you already know. You told me. You have your file."

"We know what you say. We want to know what you think. I'll be in touch."

After lunch, we said our good-byes. I went back to the bank. I didn't tell anyone about my meeting with Phillips, nor about the tests that I would be undergoing. I felt electrified—nervous and exhilarated at the same time. Suddenly, I could see myself becoming important in something as important as this was, standing up to the government, actually making a change. I wanted to do something—not so much for my country, but for my people. I'm not a patriot, per se. Not the flag-waving, José Martí kind, anyway. I saw people arrested. I saw people imprisoned. I saw what was happening to my people. And I wanted to do something about it.

The days passed slowly as I waited for Bishop to reach out to me again. By the fourth or fifth day, I began to think he wouldn't. I knew it wasn't a government trap, that he wasn't a Cuban security agent trying to test my loyalty. If he were, I would surely have been arrested right away. Perhaps as I stepped out of the Floridita. Or as I was getting up from the table. There would be no value in waiting.

No, I thought he had changed his mind. Why else would it be taking so long?

The sixth day came and went.

On the seventh, the phone in my office rang.

"I have a call for you, sir," the receptionist said when I answered. "A Mr. Bishop."

Bishop told me to meet him the next morning at a building at the corner of 23rd and O, across the street from the Hotel Nacional. Oddly, or at least it seemed so then, he told me to have the taxi drop me off a block away. When I reached the building, Bishop was already there. He met me out front. We chatted for a few moments, until a driver pulled up in a big sedan, a Lincoln or a Caddy, black. Bishop told me to get in.

The driver appeared to be another American. He greeted us in English. But after his quick "hello," he fell silent.

He drove us to an apartment building near the U.S. Embassy. He must have taken a back route, though, because I didn't see it on our way there. And I didn't see it as Bishop and I got out of the car and entered the building. Only after we were inside the apartment, some six stories up, and I looked out beyond the balcony, did I notice the embassy and realize where we were.

The building was nothing fancy. And though the apartment appeared to be completely furnished, it, too, was nothing fancy. It looked like an average apartment for an average middle-class family. It was impossible for me to tell if anybody really lived there, but it was clear that Bishop felt perfectly comfortable in it. And he clearly wasn't worried about any interruptions.

A man was waiting for us in the apartment. I don't know if he said his name or not. I don't remember. He looked about thirty-five, with blue eyes and light brown hair. He was tall, slim, with strong arms. I got the sense that he was military, or had been in the military. It turned out to be Dick Melton, a man I would see nearly daily for a month, although I would never know much more about him than his name. If it *was* his name.

Melton asked me to take off my suit jacket and took me into a back room. That's where I saw the balcony, and the U.S. Embassy beyond it. He pointed me to a wooden chair next to a table loaded with equipment.

One of the machines turned out to be a lie detector. It was a big and bulky device with a number of cryptically labeled knobs and switches. Wires trailed off it, and after I sat down, Melton connected them to me one by one. One attached to a pair of metal plates he slipped onto two of my fingers. Two rubber tubes went around my chest. Melton slipped a blood pressure cuff around my arm. I felt it fill and tighten when he turned on the machine.

"Relax," he said. "This won't hurt."

The machine hummed softly. A wide strip of paper began to move across it, under a set of pens as thin as needles that began to jiggle and leave jittery lines as the paper rolled past, like an EKG.

"Have you taken any kind of tranquilizer?" Melton asked.

"No."

Melton made a quick mark on the paper with his own pen.

"Try to remain calm," Melton continued. His Spanish was very bad, poorly pronounced and full of errors, but he insisted on speaking to me in my native tongue.

"Please answer as honestly and thoroughly as you can."

The questions were written on sheets in a loose-leaf notebook. There were several pages of them. Later I could see that he had underlined several of them. I don't know if that meant those were questions he had asked, or if those were questions where the answers had raised some issue. But the questions went on and on.

I later realized there was a science to them, to the order and manner in which he asked them. There was even a science to the design of the room. I didn't know it then, but it could have been taken straight from the CIA's own manual on interrogation techniques.

"The room in which the interrogation is to be conducted should be free of distractions," it reads. "The colors of walls, ceiling, rugs, and furniture should not be startling. Pictures should be missing or dull."

Maybe that is why I have such a hard time remembering anything beyond Melton, the machines, and the U.S. Embassy beyond the balcony.

"Good planning will prevent interruptions," the interrogation manual continues. "The effect of someone wandering in because he forgot his pen or wants to invite the interrogator to lunch can be devastating."

Some interruptions, however, are intentional.

At first, Bishop seemed uninterested in the questions. He sat in a chair by the wall and read some newspapers, rustling the pages loudly as they turned. He wandered in and out of the room.

Melton ticked off questions in the notebook. He would look at the paper, ask me a question or two, then, if something interested him, or seemed to, he might ask another question or more about my answer. Every once in a while, he scribbled a quick notation on the graph paper on the lie detector, or circled a spike on the shaky ink lines.

"Please state your full name," Melton said.

"Antonio Carlos Veciana Blanch."

"Blanch?"

"My mother's maiden name," I said. "In Cuba, we . . ."

Bishop cleared his throat. Melton moved on.

"I understand," he said. "What is your address?"

I gave it.

"Are you married?"

I nodded.

"Please answer out loud."

"Yes."

"What is your wife's name?"

He continued that way for a few more minutes, asking questions I knew he knew the answer to. Occasionally, he made another quick mark on the moving paper.

The questions moved deeper—first into my past, then into my thinking.

He asked me where I had studied. Who were the people in my circle of friends.

They already knew a lot about me. He knew I had been with the Catholic Youth Organization. He knew I had been with the Radical Liberation Movement. Later, the group became supporters of Fidel Castro. But I was just a regular member. The movement had a radio program, but I never went to speak. I only paid the monthly dues to help keep it on the air, about two pesos a month.

What did I think about the government? Did I have friends in the government?

When I mentioned Rufo López Fresquet, Bishop rustled his newspaper loudly. It startled me. Melton circled a spot on the graph paper.

"Tell me about Fresquet," Melton said. "Are you close with Fresquet?"

"Well, we don't socialize frequently."

"Does he ask for information?"

"No."

"Do you offer any?"

"No."

Melton checked off a line in the notebook.

"Who else?"

I told him about my cousin Guillermo Ruiz, who had an important job in Cuban intelligence. Melton pressed for details: Were we
close? Did I see him often? What did we talk about?

I don't know if they were already thinking it then, but I wondered
if they were trying to find out if they could get me to become part of
the government.

"Have you ever supported the government?"

"No."

"But you opposed Batista."

"Yes, but being against one dictator doesn't make me a supporter
of another."

"You think Castro is a dictator?"

"Not yet."

"You ran for president of the accountants' association."

"Yes."

"But not as a 26th of July candidate."

"No."

"Why?" Melton asked. He sounded truly perplexed. "Why would
someone like you—an accountant, at a bank—stand up to them like
that? Why make trouble for yourself?"

I hesitated a moment. The answer was complicated. Curiously, I
asked another friend of mine almost the exact same question a couple
of years later, after we had both left Cuba. He replied, "These people
don't allow you to be neutral. If you're not with them, you're against
them. They forced me to work for them. They couldn't just leave me
alone."

I was thinking the same thing sitting in that chair facing Melton.
The government pushed you, until they made you an enemy.

"They wouldn't let me be neutral," I said.

Melton paused. The lie detector needles seemed remarkably still.

"What *do* you think of the government?" Melton asked.

I hadn't yet reached the conclusion that Fidel was a Communist. I
had my doubts about him, but I hadn't arrived at that yet.

"I think they're a bunch of incompetents," I said. "Dangerous
incompetents."

The needles jumped again.

"Have you ever received any offer for a position in the government?"

I told him about Rufo's offer.

"Fresquet again."

"I turned him down."

Melton made a mark on the graph paper.

"I have sent people to go to work in the government," I continued, before he had a chance to ask another question. "Because the finance minister asked me for it."

"Friends of yours?"

"Yes."

"Still friends of yours?"

"Yes."

He made a mark.

Melton asked similarly penetrating questions about my schooling, about the rituals and rigors of the Marist school, about my religious practices. He asked about my involvement in Catholic Youth, and about other associations, clubs, and organizations I'd been a part of. About the accountants' association. About the bank, my duties there, and the people I worked with. He questioned my thinking and political leanings, my critique of the actions of current government officials, including some specifically by name, whom I knew. He asked my opinions about world politics. He asked about my favorite pastimes.

The questions seemed to go all over the place. They were curious about what I had done against Batista. Were the civic organizations I was in the kind that placed bombs or did any of that?

"No," I said. "They were groups of people in opposition to Batista, but we would only sell bonds to finance the rebels or that kind of thing."

Melton's questions about my career caught my attention. He asked about the various kinds of work I had done and the different positions I had held over the years. He was most specific about my current job at the Banco Financiero. He asked the exact time that I arrived at and left work, what kind of information I gave my supervisors.

His goal, I would later learn, was to determine my responsibilities, habits, and routines, to know the details of my life. And more. They wanted to reveal my character, my beliefs. My sympathies. My values. They wanted to assess me as a person, to evaluate me as a candidate, to judge my capability as a conspirator. They wanted to determine how sure I was about my antigovernment feelings, how much courage I would have in difficult or dangerous times, and how much imagination I had for what they wanted to do with me.

In short, to see if they could use me, and how.

The questioning continued for close to two hours. Maybe more. By the time he turned off the machine, I felt drained.

"*Gracias,*" Melton said. "You can go."

Bishop walked me to the elevator.

"Remember," he said, "you can't talk to anyone about this. You can't tell anyone. Not even your family. Nobody can know that you are in contact with us."

"I understand."

"Good," he said. "You can catch a cab outside. I'll be in touch."

He sent me down in the elevator alone.

ANOTHER WEEK WENT by before Bishop contacted me again. This time, he picked me up at the bank. The car was different. Still large, American, but maroon, not black. He drove.

We didn't go back to the apartment. He drove along the Malecón, past the U.S. Embassy, through the tunnel leading to Miramar. We continued past the luxurious homes of diplomats and the wealthy, and on into the lush greenery of Country Club. Bishop parked in front of an attractive, ranch-style home.

A different man opened the door. Not Melton. This man was taller, older. He had gray hair and thick glasses. Very thick. I don't know why, but I got the impression that he might be a doctor.

Bishop introduced him as John Smith, which I immediately took to be fictitious.

"Smith" spoke Spanish, too. Pretty well. But it was clear that he was a gringo.

"Please," he said, "have a seat." He signaled toward a La-Z-Boy recliner.

They didn't connect me to a lie detector this time, nor to any kind of equipment. This time, Smith handed me a little white pill.

"Take this," he said. "It will relax you."

I held it between my fingers a moment, thinking. I wondered what, exactly, I was being given. I was just beginning to recognize that the CIA revels in using euphemisms. For an agency that calls murder "wet work," I was sure "relax" didn't mean I was being given a tranquilizer. I suspected it was some kind of truth serum, meant to lower my inhibitions so that I would answer questions without thinking, without resisting, without deception.

"Would you like something to drink?" Smith asked. "Some water, or a soft drink?"

"No, thank you," I said. I popped the pill in my mouth and swallowed.

He waited about twenty minutes before he started asking questions. I guess they were waiting for the pill to take effect. I didn't recline. I just sat. Smith stood, chatting with me amicably about meaningless things—the weather, my drive out to the house.

After a while, he asked how I was feeling.

"Good," I said.

Actually, I felt dizzy. I hadn't thought about it until he asked, but now I realized that he had been right. I felt relaxed. Very. Woozy, yet conscious.

"Then let's begin," Smith said.

This time the questions were much more personal. There were a lot about my sexuality. Did I like women? Did I go out with women? Did I have a girlfriend, or a lover? Was I attracted to men?

"What?" I asked. "I don't understand."

"Men," Smith said. "Do you like men? Physically."

"No."

"Not at all? You don't feel anything when you see a really handsome man? Or when a very good-looking man invites you to lunch?"

"No."

He continued that way for a while. I don't remember for how long. I just remember feeling uncomfortable. I couldn't understand why he kept pressing the issue. I began to wonder if maybe Smith was attracted to men and was projecting his sentiments on me.

Suddenly, he changed tack. He began asking if I liked to drink, or do drugs. Had I ever? Did I want to? What about gambling? He asked me if I went to the casinos. I said no. I didn't believe in the lottery or any of that stuff. I would go to Club Náutico on occasion. But I didn't frequent clubs. I wasn't that kind of guy.

He asked me questions about religion. I answered honestly. I wasn't a fanatic, but at that time I still believed very strongly. I don't remember the questions clearly, but I remember they seemed to go on for a very long time. It seemed he kept asking the same things over and over again, about religion, about family, about politics, about my feelings about Cuban sovereignty.

Finally, the questions ended.

I looked at my watch. We had been at it for nearly three hours. My head was clearing. I no longer felt drunk or light-headed. I felt like I was waking from a deep sleep and that, with each passing minute, I was blinking away the grogginess of slumber.

After we finished, Bishop drove me back to the bank. We didn't talk much. He probably thought I was still feeling the effects of the drug. In fact, I kept reviewing the parts of the interrogation I recalled. Fragments of the session bubbled up in my memory, like broken pieces of flotsam rising in the sea.

By the time we reached the bank, my head was completely clear. As I stepped from the car, Bishop began to speak. I stopped him.

"I know," I said. "You'll be in touch."

He smiled.

"Yes."

TWO WEEKS LATER, Bishop called. He said he needed to get together with me in a quiet place to discuss the results of the tests. He rented a room at the Hotel Riviera. He said the meeting would probably take about two hours. It lasted more than six, until six in the afternoon. We ordered room service and ate as Bishop continued to go over my answers to the questions in minute detail.

My life was now an open book. He ticked off parts of my history that reflected his interest—delving into all the factors that influenced my personality. He commented on the different stages of my life: about my leadership in the Catholic Youth group, and my abandoning religious fanaticism.

He wanted to know what caused me to lose that faith. He asked about my affiliation with the Radical Liberation political movement I had been part of, along with several of Fidel Castro's current advisers. He asked about my time at university and about friends from my youth. He asked about my social circle, about the places I frequented, and about my work. I was perplexed about the granular detail he dredged through about my sentiments and inclinations.

After lunch, Bishop shared his concerns.

"Tony, you're an interesting case," he said. "But there are some disturbing factors."

"Like what?"

"Don't get me wrong," he answered. "You're a good prospect. You have natural talent. You have the stability and the courage to deal with difficult situations. You have the creativity to be able to switch gears when you have to, to come up with a new plan as circumstances require. You have a spirit of sacrifice, resolve, will, and ideals."

He paused.

"That last is important. We don't want to simply use people. We want to call upon men of thought and action."

"Maybe I'm not understanding," I said, "but those don't sound like negatives."

"Those aren't. Your fanaticism about family, religion, and nationalism are."

"Fanaticism?" I protested. "I don't think I'm a fanatic."

"Most fanatics don't."

I nodded. "Agreed, but still . . ."

He stopped me.

"Here's what worries me," he said. "First, religion." He raised a finger, like he was counting off a list.

"Is it a handicap that I've cooled on religion?" I interrupted.

"It's not the chilling that's unsettling," he said. "Quite the opposite. What worries me is the warmth that remains. Religious ardor can be damaging. Espionage requires an appreciation of religion. Certainly the sermons are beautiful. Religion encourages men to uphold the good and reject the bad. I agree with that."

"Then it can be a good thing."

"It can be," he said with a wry smile. "For people in other professions. A counterrevolutionary needs to be part spy, part saboteur. Scruples get in the way."

I waited for him to go on.

"We need to be able to lie, steal, and, if it comes down to it, kill." He took a swig of his drink. "And there's probably at least three or four more commandments I'd put on shaky ground. If push comes to shove."

He sighed heavily.

"You have to be willing to do whatever it takes," he continued. "Whatever. Without question. Without doubt. Without hesitation."

"I can," I said instantly, almost before he finished. "I can."

He looked at me, appraising me. Finally, he nodded.

"OK."

He raised a second finger.

"Nationalism," he said. "You wrote that article, saying the U.S. should get its stinking paws off of Cuba."

"That's not what it said," I interjected. "I was talking about the banks. I said the U.S. doesn't allow foreign banks to control its currency, for good reason. But in Cuba, they expect us to allow them. I don't think that's right. But I don't think that's nationalism. That's just good economic sense. And fair."

This time, Bishop nodded.

"Fair enough," he said. "But . . ."

He raised another finger.

"One more. Family."

"What about it?" I asked.

"What would happen if you have to go away from them for extended periods of time?"

"That's not a problem," I said. "I already do. Part of my duties as the bank's comptroller is to perform audits on all of our branches. All over the country. That takes me away for a week, two, sometimes longer."

He nodded again.

"But you already knew that," I said.

"Yes," he said. "I just wanted to be sure you did."

He smiled.

"Our tests show that you're a very passionate person," he continued. "That's good, as long as you don't lose sight of the way the world really is. Religion blinds. Family blinds. Nationalism is a dangerous devotion."

He let it sink in a moment. "You might be right when it comes to banks, but don't forget that it was the nationalist spirit of the Germans and the Japanese that led the world into the worst war man has ever known. Hitler was a nationalist fanatic."

It had obviously struck a chord. I didn't know then that as a young nose gunner on a B-17, Bishop had been shot down during World War II and wound up spending more than a year in a German prisoner-of-war camp. I didn't know that that was where he got his introduction to intelligence work, as part of the camp's escape committee. Nor that he had escaped himself and, with the help of a simple French villager, had finally made his way back to the American line.

"The nationalist philosophy is for the blind. The shortsighted. The feeble—in body or mind," he continued. "In 1952, Stalin ordered the Communists to use the nationalist flag, and ever since then they have been using it to hide behind and to confuse the gullible throughout the world."

"Maurice," I said, "just as you're proud of your country, I'm proud of mine. That is why I want to help you."

"I repeat," he responded, "it's not bad to be patriotic. But it can be dangerous to be a patriot."

He paused, choosing his words carefully before he continued.

"The first demonstrates loyalty and principles. What's bad is if it goes to excess. We can't lose sight of the fight the world is facing. These are historic times. Either we defend the man who aims for the summit of science and dignity based on honest effort, or the other side, the ones who want to impose their absurd egalitarian philosophy on the world."

"I don't see that much of a difference in our thinking, Maurice," I said. "In fact, I don't see any divergence at all."

"I just want us to be absolutely clear and avoid any misunderstandings," he said. "This is precisely the moment to put everything in its place. Later on, any discrepancies could be harmful for both parties."

He looked at his watch.

"It's late," he said.

"Wait. I have a question," I said. "If something happened to me while I'm doing my duties for you—if I had a serious accident, or died—what happens to my family? Will they get some kind of compensation, some money to take care of my kids?"

"Of course," Bishop said. "You can be sure they will be taken care of."

"I thought so," I said. "I just wanted to hear you say it."

"OK," he said. "Now go home. Think about it. I will, too. There's a lot in the balance. I'll be in touch."

NOVEMBER ARRIVED BEFORE I heard from him again. In the meantime, I thought. As he had said I should. I worried about my family. About my children. About what life would be like for them if their father wound up dead, lined up in front of a firing squad and shot as a spy, or thrown into one of Cuba's squalid prisons, never to see the light of day again.

In the end, though, I have to confess I thought more about me than about them. I felt the call of adventure, the thrilling lure of danger, the overpowering desire to overcome a childhood of slights, of standing on the sidelines wishing to be on the field, and the sense of inferiority it produced. Sadly, I admit, it was my ego that decided.

So, when Bishop called, I was ready.

He told me to come to the building across the street from the Hotel Nacional again, at 23rd and O. Now, though, I was to come inside and up to his office: "The Cuba Mining Co." I didn't speak English well enough to get the joke.

"And the taxi . . ." he began.

"A block away," I said. "I know."

The building was open. There was no doorman. I walked right in. There was a Berlitz Language School on the first floor. I didn't pay very much attention to it then, but years later, it would seem a very important clue in connecting the man who called himself Maurice Bishop and David Atlee Phillips. Even though Phillips insisted to his grave, and under oath, that he had never used that name, and that he didn't know me, he did know the Berlitz school. As my friend Gaeton Fonzi—journalist, author, and member of the investigative staff with the House Select Committee on Assassinations—wrote in *The Last Investigation*:

> Phillips admitted that after he hung up his shingle as a public rela-
> tions counselor, "No one rushed the door in any event, nor did I
> solicit clients." He noted, though, that he did eventually wind up
> with at least one client with which he briefly worked a trade for
> French lessons: the Berlitz language school.

I got on the elevator and rode up to Bishop's floor. The elevator let out onto a hallway with several offices, connected by a terrazzo floor. I found his a few doors down.

I rang the bell. Bishop opened almost immediately. The only people there were Bishop and Dick Melton. They ushered me into the small vestibule inside and closed the door.

The furnishings were modern. They looked new and rarely used. There were ashtrays around the room, as was the custom in those days, but I never saw cigarette butts in them, nor any papers in the wastebaskets. On only two future occasions, by the change in the placement of the chairs, did I get the sense that others had used the office.

There was a small sofa in the front room, but I never sat there. I got my training in the back room, at a table with two chairs. Sometimes Maurice Bishop participated. At other times he wasn't even there. Melton rarely sat.

Bishop wore a suit and tie, as usual. Melton didn't. Ever. He was always dressed casually, in shirtsleeves, with no tie.

"Rule number one," Bishop said, "try not to be seen coming in. Or leaving. You already know to have the taxi let you off a block or two away. Do the same on your way out—walk a couple of blocks before you flag a cab."

The training was supposed to take two months. Mine was cut in half. I would arrive at 9:00 a.m. and leave at ten minutes to one. That was early enough to avoid being seen by the lunchtime crowd leaving the building, but late enough that I would quickly mingle into the flock of pedestrians going about their midday business on the street.

They told me to get away from the building rapidly, but not so fast that I would arouse suspicion. They wanted me gone by the time Melton came down so I wouldn't see who was picking him up. He was a foreigner who didn't know his way around the city and depended on others for transportation.

Melton spoke a lot of Spanish, but he wasn't fluent. His language was English, and that's what he spoke to teach me. I was pretty much the opposite. So, sometimes I had to ask him to slow down so I could understand.

As time went on, it became clear that Melton was not only an educated man, but a man who liked order and thoroughness. He had a folder with all of his notes in it. As we went through each class, he was like a professor, referring to his notes constantly as he explained. In truth, I don't think he really needed them. He knew exactly what he was explaining. Perfectly. He knew the lessons by heart.

It clearly disturbed him that we had to rush through my training as fast as we did. "I don't know what kind of operative you'll be after this course," he said to me once. "Sorry about that. Maurice and I both are convinced that you have what it takes to go far. But at this rate, a lot of it is going to be up to you."

I didn't ask Melton questions. I was spellbound. Day after day, minute by minute, I listened intently as he reeled out the inner workings of his tradecraft. I was an apprentice to a form of sorcery I had never imagined—part magic, part skill, and part will—as much an art of deception and illusion as precise execution.

Melton was my master, the imparter of the conspirator's commandments. And I was determined to commit every detail to memory.

"Your job as a conspirator," he said, "is to use situation-appropriate means to create chaos within the enemy lines. Your job is to both gather information and cause damage. That might come as the result of a bomb, a fire, a bullet, or a carefully placed piece of misinformation that will disrupt the functioning of the government."

I listened carefully as Melton explained in intricate detail the methods, the tools, and the skills I needed to be effective. He repeated them again and again, like a teacher guiding his students through the alphabet for the first time.

"This is serious stuff," he said. "This is a grave matter."

The wording of the commandments was deceptively simple, easily remembered, but loaded with meaning. Each word implied insinuation. Each idea involved tactic. The combination of words and ideas represented the conduct expected of me. The limitations and capabilities were laid out perfectly in simple instructions.

I recognized the importance of each not only by the emphasis that Melton placed on it as he explained, but also later, as I reflected on them. Melton urged me to meditate upon them frequently.

- Achieve favorable opinions for your cause and critical ones for those of the enemy.
- Always maintain a double personality, disguising your real activity.
- Maintain your objectives in missions and absolute secrecy. Never reveal your associations, connections, or collaborators.
- Use whatever is necessary in your battle plan. Your enemy is perverse by nature and will not hesitate to use whatever means necessary against you.

- Mistrust people, situations, and appearances. Be on your guard all the time.

"Your enemy's best weapon is to infiltrate someone into your group," Bishop said. "They'll offer some of your associates their lives in exchange for telling them where to find you. You'll learn that silence is the friend that will never betray you."

He warned me never to fall to the temptation of expanding my circle. "You're not competing to be Miss Congeniality. Your friend and associate today could be your betrayer tomorrow."

In the eventuality that someone in my group got captured, he said, "they will be tortured. You must anticipate that they will tell everything they know. If someone you work with is arrested, you need to take every precaution. Immediately."

Your cause needs to come first, before any sentimentality.

- Be bold in your objectives. Anything is possible if you plan well enough.
- Anticipate the personal risks you're willing to take, and the cause they represent.
- Be disciplined in doing exactly the work assigned, in accordance with the instructions received.
- Maintain strict silence about your superiors and collaborators from other countries.
- Use the services of your friends and acquaintances to achieve your goals. Unscrupulously if necessary. The ends justify the means.

"Your position, your personality, your contacts," Bishop said, "could be very useful to help prevent these people from consolidating their power."

Neither Melton nor Bishop ever spoke to me about being a spy. They didn't think of me as someone who would plant bombs or anything like that. What they wanted of me was for me to wage a psychological war against the government. They didn't call it that. They called it a "propaganda campaign." To discredit the government. To disrupt the government. That was their goal.

"You're a man who can organize a resistance to disable the government," Bishop said. "So that the people understand what this government is."

I knew that was valuable, too. Because there was great confusion in the populace. I saw it in my own family. Some of my relatives, when I started expressing my doubts about the direction the government was taking, or the danger of the "socialist ideal" it was beginning to impose, called me a fool.

"You only think that way because you work with a millionaire," they said.

I did work with a millionaire. A multimillionaire. And Bishop and Melton knew that my position at Julio Lobo's bank allowed me to learn certain things about the government, and then to use that information against them. I had access, and I had the ability. I could do things to undermine them. I could use ideas to counter their ideas. Often enough, I ended up using their own ideas against them. That's what Bishop wanted. More than for me to be a terrorist. I became a terrorist later. They didn't even want to teach me about weapons. I had to ask them to.

"You're not in the military," Bishop said. "You need to be what you are—a person who knows many people and can influence many more."

"But I need to be able to defend myself, don't I? To protect myself?"

Despite the oft-repeated saying that it's better to fight and run away, Bishop insisted, "It's better not to fight at all. Avoid a direct confrontation with your enemy any time you can. Almost always, when someone in the resistance has to shoot it out with the authorities, they lose. There's more of them than there are of you."

Eventually, though, I persuaded them. A little at a time.

At first they just showed me how to break down a pistol and put it back together. Later, they taught me about explosives, and how to use them. C3, C-4, firebombs the size of cigarette packs. Easy to transport. Easy to conceal. I learned about timed fuses and detonators. How to arm and set off a bomb.

Still, I don't think they ever expected me to become a man of action. I'm not sure I did, either. Circumstances took me there.

The training they gave me prepared me. And it served me well.

Melton and Bishop insisted on offering me practical advice that they had gained through their own experience, which they knew was vital for an intelligence agent's success. I never forgot them. Abiding by those rules can save your life.

- Stop going to the places you normally frequent. If you're being followed, avoid any of the places you previously visited.
- When you walk on the street, go counter to traffic.
- Avoid meetings with more than two people.
- Don't go out at night. Don't transport weapons or explosives at night. When it's necessary, do it by day, moving during the busiest hours.
- When you travel by car, do it accompanied by a woman. Don't travel with men.
- Develop and rely on your memory. Do not take notes. If you're stopped, a little piece of paper could incriminate you.

If I did write things down, or if it was necessary to communicate in writing, they instructed me in the use of invisible ink and simple codes to obscure the information. For example, my telephone number in Cuba was 649-1226. Using one of the codes, I might reverse it and add a one to each number. Encoded, it would become 733-2057.

They also taught me that the voice is the last thing that changes in a person. People sound the same for a long time. Their looks change. Their faces change. They may gain or lose weight as they age. Their hair color changes, or their style does. They wear it longer or shorter, or they may have less of it. They wear glasses, or they replace the glasses they had with contacts. Men grow beards or mustaches, or shave them off. Ears and noses grow. But the voices rarely change. At least not until many, many years have passed.

They told me that if I wanted to remember the way someone looked, I should key in on distinctive features. Notice if someone has a mole, or a birthmark. Large ears, a large or oddly shaped nose, very close-set eyes. It not only helps your recall, it allows you to describe them to someone else succinctly. If someone told me that one of Castro's agents was missing his ring finger on his right hand, I'd be looking for it every time I shook hands with a stranger.

There were other important instructions:

- Don't take or make incriminating phone calls. Don't speak over the phone with anyone you don't know.
- Don't show up for an appointment without first reconnoitering the location to be sure everything is OK. Never go to a meeting unless you're absolutely sure that there is no problem.

That meant that even if I didn't see anything, I still wouldn't just go and knock on your door. If I needed to see you, I would communicate with you before I got there. A few minutes ahead, I might call.

I learned the value of that one within just a couple of months.

Orlando Castro, a former Communist revolutionary who fell out with Castro, was one of the people I worked with on some clandestine things. If he called me at home—this was in the days before cellular phones and caller ID, of course—he would let it ring three times, hang up, and then call back. That way I knew it was him before I picked up. If someone just let it ring and ring, I knew it was someone who didn't know me.

I also gave Orlando a countersign. If I called him, I might say something like, "May I speak with Roberto López, please?"

If he answered, "Who's calling?" I knew he wasn't alone.

One time, I was supposed to meet Orlando at one of our safe houses. Some people who had gone into exile left me the key so that we could use it. I stopped at a store with a pay phone a few blocks away and called the house. A woman answered.

I said, "May I speak with Roberto López?"

She said, "I can help you."

I hung up and walked away fast.

I went back to my car, and as I was leaving, I drove past his street. Up the block, in front of his house, I saw several patrol cars. He had been arrested. Someone in his group had tipped off state security.

The government agents were playing it smart. They knew he wasn't working alone. So they had someone sitting by his phone, taking calls, looking to see who else they could round up.

I never went back to that house.

- Dress in a normal, unassuming fashion. Don't wear clothes or colors that call attention to you. Don't wear dark glasses.
- Wear a hat or a cap to hide the shape of your head, but don't make it a very conspicuous one.
- Learn to disguise yourself with a mustache or a beard that you can grow or change. The same man can look completely different with a goatee, a full beard, or an Amish one. The same with a pencil mustache, or a thick one.

One day, after my lesson ended and I was getting ready to leave, Bishop asked me to wait. He spoke very somberly as he said, "Tony, you need to understand that this isn't about showing how brave you are. For an undercover agent, there are times that the best route is to run away. Even if they call you a coward. You cannot let them arrest you."

He took a capsule from his pocket and handed it to me.

"If your capture is inevitable, take this. It's poison. Deadly in seconds. We'll take care of your family."

I took the capsule and nodded. "I will. I swear."

chapter 5
PATIENCE AND TIME
DO MORE THAN VIOLENCE

I CARRIED THE suicide pill with me at all times. If anybody had seen it and asked, I probably would have told them it was heart medicine. It was. To stop it.

So it rested safely in my pocket as I completed my training, and after, as I went about my duties at the bank. Bishop and I agreed that my position was of the utmost importance to accomplish the mission expected of me. It gave me access to valuable economic information and allowed me to maintain contact with powerful members of the financial community.

We didn't know then that it would also bring me face-to-face with Che Guevara, and his gun.

TO MINIMIZE THE chance of being discovered, my meetings with Bishop became increasingly infrequent once my training ended, until they were virtually nonexistent. We communicated only when absolutely necessary, and then mostly through messages written in invisible ink, hidden in letters sent to an intermediary's address in the name of Caridad Rodríguez. Anyone reading any of them would have been impressed at how dutiful and loving Caridad and her cousin Adolfina, who lived in the United States, continued to be with each other, and how lovely their handwriting was. As I ironed them, though, the heat brought out Bishop's hidden message.

After I read them, I destroyed the letters.

That became our only means of communication barely six months after I first met him. Bishop came and went from the island somewhat frequently during those months. In March 1960, he left Cuba for good.

"It's getting too hot," he told me as he prepared to leave. He didn't mean the temperature. Tensions between Cuba and the United States were increasing steadily. And as opposition against the government grew, so did the repressive security aimed at stopping it.

Before he left Cuba—I'll never forget—he tore twelve American dollar bills in half and handed one set of the halves to me.

"Hold on to those," he said. "If someone comes to you and they say they're speaking for me, or they have a message from me, they'll have to give you one of these halves. If they don't have one, or if the one they give you doesn't match one that you have, they're lying. It's a trap. Don't tell them anything, and get away as fast as you can."

BISHOP HAD READ the tea leaves well. Not too long after he left, Castro's agents arrested two FBI agents assigned to the U.S. Embassy, Edwin Sweet and William Friedemann, as they left a meeting of counter-revolutionaries. They were charged with "encouraging terrorist acts," among other things, and expelled immediately.

Things were indeed getting hot. But, as usual, there was another reason Bishop pulled up stakes so suddenly. One he kept secret from me. In fact, Bishop had been summoned back to Washington to begin preparations for an operation that would go down in history as one the most colossal CIA failures of all time, the Bay of Pigs. The failed invasion would also put him on a collision course with the man who would soon be the country's next president, John F. Kennedy.

Within days of Bishop's departure, the current president, Dwight Eisenhower, officially approved the covert action plan against Castro.

In addition to authorizing the buildup of the paramilitary invasion force, Eisenhower approved a "powerful propaganda campaign" aimed at weakening support for Fidel.

The task force to run the anti-Castro operation was formed at a meeting in Washington on January 18, 1960. The attendees included David Atlee Phillips.

In his book, he talks about being called back to Washington in March to take charge of the propaganda phase of the campaign. In doing so, he fell back on tactics that he and his agency colleagues had used to help topple Guatemalan President Jacobo Árbenz in 1954, establishing a CIA-run radio station to beam anti-Castro messages at the island. Radio Swan went on the air May 17.

Before Bishop left, though, he went to great lengths to impart valuable lessons about his craft, along with lengthy discourses about his views of it.

"The secret agent's function has taken on an immeasurable worth in modern times," he told me once, during one of our final training sessions. "The atomic age and scientific espionage techniques have changed the game completely. They've also changed the ways of conquering nations."

"We still use armies," I said.

"Yes," he said. "Men with guns, yes. But armed conflicts run the risk of escalating. The threat of nuclear war, and the catastrophic devastation that would result, is too great. We start lobbing modern atomic weapons at each other, and the Stone Age will seem like advanced technology."

"What about Korea?"

"Limited wars are still a possibility," he said, "but the best option of all is psychological warfare."

Even before I could consider too deeply the various ways that might take shape, Bishop launched into the core of that day's lesson.

A conspirator's duties include a variety of objectives, he explained. His principal work is not gathering intelligence, but more to intelligently influence events to impact public opinion. The goal is to eliminate enemies and benefit friends. Undercover operations are excellent methods for achieving those goals, especially if we're able to avoid being publicly tied to those efforts.

"The success of a clandestine operation requires just that, that it remain clandestine—secret, invisible, unknown," Bishop said. "The result should appear completely unconnected to any of our actions. That's why it's of the utmost importance to not leave tracks or compromising evidence of any kind.

"But even if you do, remember," he added, "we will forever deny our involvement. Forever. Even when it's obvious."

Secrecy, he insisted, was absolute.

"We don't get to be heroes," he said. "No one ever knows what we do. Your triumphs won't be applauded in the newspapers. The president doesn't shake your hand on the evening news. Our satisfaction comes from doing our duty. It comes from knowing you helped your friends and hurt your enemies, even if no one else ever knows."

An operative's main goal is to divide and confuse the enemy.

To carry out a mission, an agent always needs to think of alternatives. He has to have backup plans. Success depends on his capacity for planning and his capability for execution. He needs to plan, prepare, perform—and expect the unexpected. For that reason, he should frequently evaluate the status of his plan and analyze his progress and consider any obstacles that have arisen.

People are his tools, and his targets. They are to be used as means to his ends. If your interests align, they're allies. If they have no interest, they're instruments. If they oppose your interests, they're enemies.

"It doesn't matter," Bishop said. "Any of them can be useful, in the right situation. If you need them, you use them. You just have to find their weakness. Everyone has one. That's the key."

He was right. Before I would "work" somebody, I had to prodigiously study their situation, their qualities, their defects. Everyone is penetrable. We just have to discover their weakness. There are those who cooperate because an alluring woman offers her bed. Others can't resist the temptation of a bundle of cash, or the promise of power. Others just need their egos stroked. One way or another, anyone can be bought.

And once their usefulness is at an end, they can be discarded. Or eliminated.

An operative's methods should not be classified as dirty or clean, he said. They are simply favorable or contrary to our cause. There are no illegitimate means. Anyone who lets his moral judgment affect his mission is, at best, a bad agent. At worst, he's a dead one.

His arsenal: lies, deceit, intrigue, theft, kidnapping, bribery, corruption, destabilization, subversion, and murder.

As I listened to his commentaries and observations, I came to understand that Bishop had a disturbingly dark view of the world. It seemed, at times, worse than Machiavellian.

I came to believe that he considered himself above the law, beyond the rules the rest of us are expected to abide by. And I came to suspect that he might have been right, that he knew something I didn't. I came to think that there is a parallel power at work in empires, that sets its own rules, for its own ends. We're all aware of the political authority that formally governs the country we live in. But Bishop made me see that outside this traditional, visible authority there is an invisible power acting in the shadows, directing events. These are the true puppet masters on the world stage, shaping the course of history. Political authority changes hands with elections. However, the true power lies in the hands of a hidden consortium that acts as an unseen overlord, watching over and deciding civilization's destiny. This "invisible directorate," this "shadow government," is politically, economically, and militarily powerful. Yet its members are not driven by ostentatious vanity. They see themselves as being tasked with a tremendous responsibility. And they are resolute. They will destroy any of the visible political leaders if they prove inconvenient to what the shadow directorates believe the national destiny should be. This secret empire of power is extensive. And it never ends, unless the country itself is destroyed. It passes from generation to generation, forever hidden, yet forever in control.

That realization led me to questions that have haunted me ever since: What was Maurice Bishop's assigned role in all of this? Was he merely a supervisor in charge of my recruitment and training? Was he working for the government—or for some force above it? For that matter, was the CIA serving America's elected leadership—or some higher authority?

I never knew. Over the years, I learned that Bishop was a very important person, with considerable connections. But I came to wonder if the ends that justified his means were ones the United States government truly knew about and approved.

"The only advantage of playing with fire," Bishop said, "is learning not to get burned."

As we neared the one-year anniversary of the regime's coming to power, Bishop made me an unexpected proposal. He asked me if I was willing to infiltrate the ranks of Castro's regime. He thought that my personal and professional history, combined with my knowledge of banking and economics, would make me an ideal candidate for an important position. I had existing relationships with people who were now key government figures. And, as president of the accountants' association, which now had been taken over by the July 26 Movement, I developed more. With my professional credentials and connections like those, Bishop said, it shouldn't be difficult to climb to key positions of the Communist government.

The objective was obvious. Becoming a part of the government would permit me to inform the CIA in advance of Castro's plans and intentions. Bishop clarified that the purpose would not be to burn me at some point, but rather to keep me infiltrated indefinitely within the orbit of the Cuban regime's leaders. Success would depend on my ability to feign loyalty to the government's doctrines. Convincingly. I would have to appear to be one of them for an indeterminate time. My acting skills and composure would be my only protections against being discovered. Bishop promised not to pressure me for information. My role would not be to ferret out military secrets or perform any sort of skulduggery. All I would need to do was keep my eyes and ears open and report the goings-on around me. The real benefit would be long-term. Presumably, the higher I would go, the more valuable the information I would be exposed to.

My mission would be known as "Operation Eagle."

I won't deny that the proposition was enticing. But it was also extremely risky. It came accompanied by a formal promise of a hefty financial reward and, if anything happened to me, the assurance that my family would be well taken care of.

On the other hand, I would be, in John le Carré's terms, "out in the cold." I couldn't count on protection of any sort. If possible, I would be warned of impending danger. But Bishop could promise nothing more. If I were captured, there would be no hope of rescue.

"Commando teams and submarines are the stuff of Hollywood films," Bishop said. "You need to be aware that your only shields are your own intelligence and your ability to deceive."

He also made it clear that under no circumstances could I reveal my secret, not even to my own family. There could be no exceptions, no matter how grave the danger. I had to take my secret to my death, even if that meant facing a firing squad.

"There's no question it would be dangerous," Bishop said, "but you would be doing a great service for your country, and your countrymen. Think about it."

I didn't have to.

I immediately began exploring ways to insinuate myself in the government. As president of the accountants' association I was, technically, a member of the July 26 Movement. That entitled me to enroll in the political school maintained by the government to instruct leaders of the militia. I went to a few meetings. I also made contact with some government officials. Using the pretext of building a rural school in the name of my dear friend Boris Luis Santa Coloma, I met with Haydée Santamaría and her husband, Armando Hart. They had both been close to Boris, as well. In fact, according to the official account of the attack on the Moncada Barracks, Boris had been captured while trying to help them escape. Now they were both members of Castro's inner circle.

My charade might've been more successful than I suspected. Later, an internal CIA memorandum surfaced. Unbeknownst to me,

Julio Lobo had been supplying information to the agency, as well. Apparently, they valued his opinion regarding a variety of matters, including me.

The communiqué "To: Havana" "From: Director" states:

JULIO LOBO PERSONAL OPINION OF VECIANA FAVORABLE DESPITE FEELING ON PART SOME IN CUBAN BANKING CIRCLES THAT VECIANA MAY BE IN SERVICE OF G 2. LOBO FEELS VECIANA NECESSARILY WALKED VERY NARROW CHALK LINE WHICH MADE HIM SUSPECT. VECIANA WAS CHOSEN ADMINISTER FUND FOR UNDERGROUND WHICH BANKERS AGREED TO ESTABLISH BUT BANK TAKEN OVER BEFORE IT SET UP.

As I moved forward, however, I became increasingly uneasy with the path I had chosen. I spent hours and hours with my agitated thoughts roiling in my brain. It wasn't fear. Not for me, anyway. I feared for my children. I feared for what my decision would do to them. One afternoon as I played with them, my wife said something that pierced me like a stake through the heart.

"I never want to see them enslaved by a totalitarian and atheist philosophy," she said.

I spent many sleepless nights agonizing over my promise to Bishop and my desire to help Cuba, and my duty to them. It was one thing to maintain a double personality to hide my intelligence work against the government, but quite another to pass myself off as one of them. I would have to hide the truth from everyone, including my children. I was terrified to think that my children would not know the difference, that they would come to identify with the Communist ideology because they were convinced that that was how their father thought.

I decided I had no option. I was willing to risk myself, but I didn't have the right to gamble with my children's future.

It had been easy to accept Bishop's proposal; telling him I had changed my mind was not. He paled when I told him of my decision, and it took a visible effort for him to gather himself.

"I understand," he finally said. I could hear the disappointment in his voice. "We'll stick with psychological warfare."

In that moment, neither he nor I could anticipate just how successful those efforts would be.

"An operative must be creative," Bishop had told me. "An undercover agent who lacks a fertile imagination is like a soldier without a gun."

Looking back on what was accomplished, I surprised even myself with how I seized upon opportunities to wreak havoc on Castro's regime.

I didn't know about Bishop's public relations and propaganda background then, but his emphasis on the power of rumors, messages, and "official" disseminations was unmistakable.

Psychological warfare, he had said, can take many forms and have many objectives. Mine aimed at economic sabotage. I knew that a carefully crafted campaign of gossip and falsehoods about the country's economic policies could have an impact significantly greater than bombs.

The destruction of the public's confidence is a science. When conditions are favorable, the magnitude of the damage that can be done is incredible. I understood the workings of economics far beyond its basic elements. It was my forte. It helped my ascent through the ranks of the banks where I had worked, and elevated me to the trusted and relatively prestigious position I now held. Now it gave me an advantage, and a weapon.

There is nothing more sensitive than capital. The consequences of its flight from a country can cause losses greater than those from an armed invasion. People may not understand economics, but they fear the disastrous fallout from the devaluation of their currency. A frightened business community would spread panic through the country at large. The multiplier effect would turn the ripple into a tidal wave. The

result: chaos. Soldiers use guns and grenades. Devaluation and inflation can be even more devastating weapons of mass destruction.

Exactly how to do it remained a question. It's one thing to understand the rules of the game and how it's played, and a totally different
one to actually step onto the field. Especially if I intended to be more
than a simple player moving at the direction of others, and instead
purported to take control.

I spent months analyzing financial statistics, market movements,
business trends, foreign trade, exchange rates, and all of the minutiae
that comprise the functioning of a nation's economy. Time was of the
essence, but I also knew the truth of Bishop's dictum that "patience
and time do more than violence." I also had to deepen and expand my
knowledge of "applied psychology" and look for ways to better adapt
its methods for my needs.

An effective campaign of rumors, apocryphal circulars, and false
information must be planned in accordance with the idiosyncrasies of
its audience. There's no magic formula. It takes an understanding of
the people, their character, and their circumstances, and then targeting
the weaknesses that would chip away at their confidence.

Turbulence and change gave us an advantage. The country had just
gone through rebellion, fighting, and the ousting of a dictator. The new
government was still finding its way. We had been through five presidents in almost as many months, and cabinet ministers seemed caught
in a revolving door. Castro introduced a host of new institutions and,
almost daily it seemed, new laws.

The result was a climate of pervasive uncertainty. Since no one
knew what new mandate the day would bring, no one knew what to
believe. Thus, in an Orwellian twist, they would believe anything.

Then, in 1960, the government's pretenses fell away, and it tilted
openly toward Communism. A stunned middle class began to accept
any information emanating from opposition sources as good and,
more important, credible.

The time, I realized, was ripe. The first campaign in the psychological war became obvious. Everyone expected some sort of currency
devaluation, or an outright confiscation of their money. That made it

feasible to spark a run on banks, eroding the people's confidence in the money in circulation and causing a financial panic.

A similar outbreak of economic anxiety, brought on by the stock markets' plummet on Black Tuesday, spurred the run on banks that marked the start of the Great Depression in the United States. I might not hope for such a calamitous impact, but at the very least I did anticipate a thundering domino effect. As people lost faith that their money would hold its value, they'd rush to buy goods while their pesos still could. That, in turn, would fuel runaway inflation.

The economy would hemorrhage.

People kept coming to me at the bank, business people, the wealthy, asking how they could get American dollars, or how they could get their money out of the country. They were nervous. They told me so. They expected an economic crisis. They didn't know if it would come because of the government's ineptitude or because of the government's deliberate actions, but they expected some kind of financial bombshell.

That gave me the idea.

I turned to people I knew, two attorneys who worked for the finance ministry. Both had participated in the drafting of the regime's laws and regulations during the first months of Castro's government. One was an uncle, who lived next door to me in La Víbora, Jorge Lamas. The other, I can't name.

I knew they could do it. They were high-level insiders. Lamas had proven it to me before.

As James O'Connor later noted: "Few people outside of Castro's immediate circle could have known the exact provisions of the first Agrarian Reform Law before it was announced on May 17, 1959. Public debate was avoided and the decree was drafted by men who did not have Cabinet positions."

Lamas knew. He told me before Castro announced it. So, as I hit upon my plan in the fall of 1960, I went to him.

"I need you to create a law that says that the government is going to confiscate the people's money," I told him. "And that the money that's on the street is going to be exchanged."

I wasn't disappointed. Lamas and his colleague worked diligently and enthusiastically for a period of two weeks. They came back with a document that looked so perfect that if I hadn't been the one who came up with the idea, I would've believed it myself. They had typed it up on the government's official letterhead, with the carefully crafted wording that was the hallmark of legislation. The only things missing were a signature and official seal. Their absence, however, actually served to further the deception—it appeared to be a draft of a new law, obtained on its way for review.

That's what I told people as we passed it out: "It was stolen from the National Bank just before it was signed."

Another trusted friend printed thousands of copies, and we handed them out to various counterrevolutionary groups to distribute.

People believed it, all over the country. Long lines formed at the banks as people demanded their money. They withdrew millions. The government was forced to respond. The very next day, President Dorticós went on television to tell the people it was a hoax. Cruel stooges of the previous administration, Batistianos, had inflicted this harm upon the Cuban people, he insisted. No such law existed, he said. No such law was being contemplated.

He was right about its existence, and possibly about whether such an idea was under consideration. At the moment. In the increasingly surreal reality that was Cuba under its new leaders, the government did almost exactly what my fake law proposed ten months later. In August 1961, Castro announced that bank accounts were being frozen and a new currency was being introduced. The existing currency was now worthless.

The change, the authorities said, was necessary "to impede that national monetary resources in the hands of the external counterrevolution be utilized to conspire against the Revolutionary Government of the people of Cuba."

Money had always been a challenge for the opposition groups, even before the "monetary reform." We needed automobiles to move around. We needed houses where people could hide.

I asked Bishop for one million pesos.

"I can't help you," he said. "You have to get it yourself."

I couldn't believe it. A million pesos—about $50,000 at the time—sounds like a lot, and it was to us, but not to Bishop. We knew that the Americans were infiltrating people onto the island and handing them that kind of money and more all the time.

Luckily for us, another member of the underground, Antonio García Álvarez, came up with a way to get it that not only helped us, but hurt the government, as well.

Some of the clandestine groups had already begun audacious assaults on banks as a means of getting the funds they needed. They staged boldly executed armed robberies, in full daylight, during regular banking hours. And, while an individual theft might not yield significant amounts, it had an oversized impact. The idea that armed guerrilla fighters could charge into any bank at any time, waving guns and screaming orders, caused a disquieting tension for anyone who had to do business in one—employees, guards, and customers. The fact that the government seemed incapable of preventing the robberies eroded the public's faith in the regime's ability to perform one of the basic functions of any government, to protect its people.

As beneficial as that was for us, we needed substantially greater sums of hard cash. García Álvarez came up with a plan to get the government to, quite literally, hand it to us. He worked at the National Institute for Agrarian Reform, which was headed by Che Guevara. With the help of Rafael Dalmau, García Álvarez fixed it so that a six-figure check made out to one of the newly nationalized companies wound up on Guevara's desk. Che dutifully stamped it with his signature. Presumably, the funds were necessary to avoid a shutdown. In reality, the enterprise didn't exist. It never had. They made up the name, manufactured the necessary documentation, and got Guevara to sign off on the check.

Another member of the underground, Roberto Vale, facilitated the rest of the con. Vale worked at a bank. He authorized the opening of an account at one of the branches he was in charge of, in the names of two fake "militants."

Every week, the two went to the bank, presented their fake IDs, and withdrew large sums of cash. To help further the charade, they carried a list of amounts that needed to be tallied, supposedly in order to pay the salaries of the company's nonexistent workers.

El Che had been named head of the Banco Nacional in November 1959. It seemed a clear signal that the government was preparing to make giant changes. Putting its most openly avowed Communist at the head of the banking system surely meant Castro's regime intended to convert its capitalist institutions to a controlled, state-run form. Since that Communist also happened to have no background in economics, the shift would most certainly be worse than wrenching. It was like putting a chemist at the controls of a plane. As capable, even brilliant, as Che Guevara might be as a revolutionary, he had no idea how to manage a system as complex as a nation's economy.

Some months after his appointment, I received a call. His secretary said El Che wanted to see me.

We met in his office at the Banco Nacional. I had only seen him in photographs and on TV before. He had a penetrating look and seemed intent on discovering my innermost thoughts. Unlike Fidel, who was a loquacious whirlwind, Che spoke softly, appearing to weigh each word carefully. He noted that he had information about me, perhaps not every detail, but certainly the principal points. After a few minutes of chitchat, he put his feet up on the desk, took his gun from his holster, and set it on the desk as well, close at hand, where I could see it.

He tactfully verified my personal information—where I came from, the functions I carried out in the civic institutions that opposed Batista's dictatorship, my position within Julio Lobo's organization, my studies and specialties, my position as a practicing Catholic.

"I understand that you, too, suffer from asthma," he said. "Have you found any medicines that give you relief? That help you breathe?"

"It was worse when I was younger," I told him. "But I found tremendous success with a French product, Lancerot."

"I'll make a note of it. Thank you," he said. "I've been using cortisone to relieve the suffering, but I know the side effects are dangerous."

"It's truly a challenging disease," I said. "I would wish it on no one. But the truth is, dealing with asthma has taught me discipline and willpower."

His face softened. El Che had been chilly and businesslike until then. Now, he smiled.

"Very true," he said. "It is an extremely severe teacher, but the lessons are valuable."

At that point, Guevara began to comment on aspects of the national economy. As he explained his theories and suggested the solutions he believed were necessary, I grew increasingly perplexed, and concerned. The suspicions that had begun nagging me when he was put in charge of the bank were now confirmed. El Che was renowned as a bold and daring man, but he was clearly illiterate in matters of economics.

I could tell he had a special interest in me. I just didn't know what. He had a reputation as a frank man who liked telling the truth, but on this occasion, he continued to withhold his reasons for summoning me. He suggested that I should cooperate with the revolution.

"We need capable and trustworthy people," he said. "You're president of the accountants' association. You enjoy good relations in economic circles. You have ample connections within banking circles. And you are a member of the inner circle of Julio Lobo's organization."

Now I understood. He wanted to use me in the regime's efforts to confiscate banks, businesses, and industries. I thought it better to let him continue without letting on that I suspected his purpose.

"Veciana, you're a young man," he said. "The same age as me. You belong to the middle class, but you mustn't forget your humble beginnings. Speaking frankly, I don't understand how you use your knowledge and your capacity to enrich those who exploit the people, especially the poor."

He paused, gauging my reaction. I made an effort to keep my face blank.

"I find it even more incomprehensible that you're religious," he continued. "Religion is the opiate of the masses. Its only purpose is to enslave the poor."

Again, he waited for a response. Again, I gave none.

"I know," he said. "My mother studied in a Catholic school. I lived the hypocrisy of the clergy. In this life, paradise is for the rich, and hell for the poor. The God that religions show us is an invention whose predetermined purpose is to dupe the gullible.

"It's a myth," he continued, gathering steam. "Life begins when we're born and ends when we die. Humans live with the false illusion of eternal life after death. Religion lulls the poor so that they'll accept their misery in this life. It's a tool of the rich and powerful to pacify the masses."

He continued this way for a while. I didn't interrupt.

"Jesus Christ is not the Son of God," he said. "He was merely a great revolutionary who wished to reform the corrupt society of his age. His first followers were valiant rebels who paid with their lives in defense of their ideals."

He seemed finally to have exhausted his discourse. He waited for me to respond.

"*Comandante*," I said, "I was raised a Catholic. I was taught to venerate a God who so loved the world he made himself flesh and bone. They made me believe God is an eternal being. I sought protection in his power."

El Che listened intently.

"But," I continued, "what I saw in the world around me made it difficult for me to believe in the God I had been taught about. I began to doubt. My faith faded, little by little, until none was left.

"After that, I only pretended to believe, to please my friends and relatives who still believed in that God. I came to the conclusion that blind faith is not wanting to accept the truth."

He seemed even more interested now. The hint of a smile played at the corners of his mouth.

"In the end, I concluded that the only truth is reality," I said.

More than two hours had gone by. El Che still hadn't told me why he asked me to meet with him, or what he wanted to propose. Just when I thought he would, his phone rang. The call apparently came from the Presidential Palace.

"My apologies," he said as he hung up. "I'm needed."

He pulled out his appointment book and scanned his agenda. "Can we meet again in two days?" he asked. "At ten?"

"At ten in the morning?" I responded. "Of course."

"Ten at night," he said. "The days are busy, and long. The revolution's needs demand it. But you are very important to me, and I would hate to put our meeting off longer than I have to."

"Of course," I said, hiding my dismay. "At ten, then, night after tomorrow. I'll be here"

I arrived promptly for our second meeting. He didn't. I waited in the bank's lobby until he marched in an hour later. He made no apology for the delay, or for his dirty uniform. By the looks of it, I guessed it was the same one he had worn to our meeting two days before, and had worn ever since.

This time, El Che appeared tired. He went straight to the point.

"Veciana, I need a list of approximately one thousand accountants willing to volunteer their time for the revolution."

"May I ask what kind of work, and for how long?"

"Let's say for six months," he said. "Administering enterprises."

I inhaled. I was right. The regime intended to seize private enterprises throughout the country and put them under government control. The other thought that struck me almost simultaneously was about the peculiar absurdity, and irony, of the situation. It appeared that even if I had not been working actively in the underground against the new government, I seemed to be unable to avoid confrontations with it.

Castro had been in power little more than a year, and here I was again faced with having to say no to a request from a government official. And not just any official: El Che himself. I answered as diplomatically as possible.

"*Comandante,*" I began carefully, "you present an extremely difficult situation. I doubt that my colleagues would be able to assume even such an important responsibility for free. Their patriotism notwithstanding, the challenges of maintaining their families create inescapable demands."

His face darkened as I continued.

"I'm afraid it would be impossible for me to find that number of accountants under those conditions," I said.

His face hardened.

"I knew I couldn't count on the accountants for help," he said. His tone became icy. "How curious the contradictions of life, don't you think? You, a common laborer's son, a child of the working class who was poor himself until just a few years ago, surrenders his intelligence and his ability to that dinosaur, Julio Lobo. I can assure you that there is no room in the new socialist Cuba for your master, Julio Lobo. Nor any of his ilk."

Yet again, I couldn't help but be amazed at how clumsy the members of the regime were. How quickly they resorted to threats to force cooperation. They preferred intimidation to invitations.

"We are greatly interested in Julio Lobo's extensive enterprises, Veciana," he continued. "Your cooperation would be extremely valuable. Providing us with inside information about the true extent of his operations and how they are administered would be greatly appreciated."

"It's a very interesting proposition, *Comandante*," I said. "Please allow me a few days to think about what I can do."

"Good! Good!" he said. "It's up to us all to do what we can for Cuba."

"How right you are, *Comandante*," I said. "How right you are."

chapter 6
CHANGE OF STRATEGY

SOMETIMES YOU PLAY with fire and nothing happens. Sometimes horrible things do. After Bishop left, both did.

I became an irresponsible risk-taker. After the meeting with Che Guevara, I took it upon myself to warn the owners of the private banks about what I expected to be the imminent government confiscation plan. It was dangerous, I knew. The regime was tightening its grip, and to be accused as a counterrevolutionary meant a summary trial followed, almost surely, by a firing squad.

I went ahead anyway.

I stuck to the rules I'd been taught, never meeting with more than two at a time. I was as cautious as possible, never giving my real reason for wanting to see them until after we were behind closed doors. Only then would I explain my purpose, and offer my warning. Never stating where I had gained the information, I told them that I believed that the government was about to step up its program of nationalization.

The warning signs had come throughout the summer. They appeared, at first, to be part of a dangerous tit for tat between the United States and Cuba. As tensions escalated, Shell, Esso, and Texaco refused to refine shipments of Soviet oil arriving on the island. Cuba responded by nationalizing their oil refineries.

At the beginning of July, Cuba upped the ante, taking control of all U.S.-owned businesses and commercial property.

I warned the bankers that the same was coming for Cuban companies. Once it happened, I told them, it would be too late. I suggested that they leave the country and withdraw the funds they maintained in foreign accounts. From my perspective, it would serve a dual purpose. It was a way for them to avoid losing their capital, and at the same time, a means of denying those funds to the Cuban government.

They all listened intently, nodded sagely, and then ignored me. I'm sure they each had what they saw as very good reasons, which none of them shared with me. I'm sure that later, they each had their own regrets.

I probably should not have hoped, much less expected, that my actions would escape the attention of the government. I know that El Che found out in fairly short order. An indiscreet banker mentioned it to one of his employees. He didn't know that the man's son had fallen ardently under the sway of the revolutionary ideology and had then succeeded in convincing his father of its merits. The employee told El Che.

However, as Guevara himself had noted, "How curious the contradictions of life."

For reasons I might never understand, El Che did nothing. Perhaps, since nothing had come of my suggestions to the bankers, he felt there was insufficient evidence to accuse me. Perhaps, since nothing had come of my telling them, he allowed me to remain free so that I could serve as an example of how futile counterrevolutionary efforts could be. Perhaps he took some sadistic pleasure in thinking that I would spend the rest of my days looking over my shoulder, wondering when my arrest would come. Perhaps all of those reasons played a part.

I think it might've been something else, though. I honestly believe that in the course of my two lengthy meetings with El Che, we actually established a rapport. I think the fact that we both suffered from asthma, both knew its pains and woes, and both had become stronger because of it gave us something in common. I think, perhaps, my admission that I had lost my faith in religion showed that we shared other things, as well.

Whatever the reason, my actions were of absolutely no importance to Guevara. He didn't lift a finger. El Che was never known for being generous with his adversaries. He was with me.

But, as I had anticipated, the government began nationalizing Cuban-owned enterprises in September. In mid-month, it seized sixteen cigar factories, fourteen cigarette plants, and twenty tobacco warehouses. Two days later, it nationalized all the U.S. banks on the island, including the First National City Bank of New York, First National Bank of Boston, and Chase Manhattan Bank.

Then came what I had warned the Cuban bankers about. On October 13, the government announced laws 890 and 891 authorizing the official takeover of all but two private banks and 382 industrial and commercial companies, along with all of their factories, warehouses, depots, property, and rights. The list included 105 sugar mills, eighteen distilleries, six alcoholic beverage companies, seven food processors, two oil and fats companies, three soap and perfume factories, five dairies, two chocolate factories, nine packaging manufacturers, sixty textile and clothing companies, three paint producers, three chemical companies, seven paper mills, six basic metallurgical companies, one flour mill, sixteen rice processors, forty-seven household goods warehouses, ten coffee roasters, three drug companies, thirteen department stores, eight railroad companies, one printer, eleven movie theater chains, nineteen construction companies, one electrical company, and thirteen maritime shippers.

I struck back that same month.

The run on banks had been successful. It taught me an effective formula. These were volatile times in Cuba. The people's apprehension was palpable. The streets buzzed with gossip and rumors about what the government might do next. The anxiety they felt about their pesos losing value had given me the idea for the fake monetary law. Now many Cuban parents worried openly about their children, about what the government might be planning for them.

They saw worrisome signs that their kids were being indoctrinated. Every classroom now had a picture of Fidel Castro on the wall. By decree. Teachers taught the kids about the glory of the revolution, about the heroic sacrifices of the fighters in the Sierra Maestra, and how they freed the people from a brutal dictatorship. The basic elements of the history lessons were fact, but the form of the instruction exalted the "Supreme Leader" in distressing ways.

Parents grew nervous that their children were being brainwashed. They wondered why. They worried about the government's intentions.

And they were primed to believe anything.

I went to an accountant I knew, Andrés Cayón, and told him what I had in mind.

"Andrés," I said, "I want to bring out a law that says the government is going to terminate parental rights. That they're going to take this authority away from mothers and fathers and assume legal custody of their children."

"What will you accomplish with that?"

"I don't know," I answered, honestly. I didn't. But I knew that good horror movies don't scare people—they prompt them to use their imaginations. People scare themselves. That's why they're afraid of the dark. They don't know what's there, or what might happen. A law that said the government was going to take control of the children, but didn't offer any specifics, would have the same effect.

"I don't know," I said again. "Let's find out."

We did it the same way as we had with the monetary law. Cayón got two people to draw up an official-looking piece of legislation. We printed thousands of copies and let the underground network filter it onto the streets.

The impact was enormous. It sparked "Operation Pedro Pan," the exodus of more than fourteen thousand unaccompanied children sent out of Cuba by their parents with the help of the Catholic Church. Monsignor Bryan Walsh, the head of the Catholic Welfare Bureau in Miami, worked with the State Department to secure visas for the children and provided care for them when they arrived.

In his account of the program's history, Walsh wrote,

> Purported copies of a new decree circulated throughout underground circles. According to this decree (as rumored) "all children will remain with their parents until they are three years old, after which they must be entrusted for physical and mental education to the Organización de Circulos Infantiles" [state day-care centers]. Children from 3 to 10 would live in government dormitories in their

home provinces and would be permitted to visit their parents "no less than two days a month." Older children would be "assigned to the most appropriate place" and thus might never come home.

I did not tell Bishop of my plan before it was in motion. I didn't have to. The CIA's Radio Swan, under David Atlee Phillips's direction, helped fan the flames. As soon as the *Patria Potestad* "law" began circulating, it began broadcasting a message: "Cuban mothers, don't let them take your children away! The Revolutionary Government will take them away from you when they turn five and will keep them until they are eighteen."

The message aired repeatedly in the coming days and weeks.

An explosion of terrifying rumors followed. Walsh later enumerated them: ". . . that children were picked up off the streets and never seen again; that orphanages, such as 'Casa Beneficencia,' had been emptied and all the children sent to Russia for indoctrination; that in the town of Bayamo, fifty mothers had signed a pact to kill their children rather than hand them over to Castro; etc."

Castro himself decried the law as a forgery but only helped further the rumors when he sent his own twelve-year-old son, Fidelito, to Russia. Then, when the government started the Juventud Rebelde (Rebel Youth) and Pioneros (Rebel Pioneers) programs, it fed parents' fears even more.

Pedro Pan began with a trickle. The first two kids, a brother and sister named Sixto and Vivian Aquino, arrived at Miami International Airport aboard Pan American World Airways flight 422 at 4:30 p.m. on December 26, 1960. By the time commercial flights between Havana and Miami stopped, ending the exodus in October 1962, the flow had become a flood, with hundreds of children arriving every month.

It had been named fancifully, a play on the tale of Peter Pan, who fled the world of grown-ups with his crew of Lost Boys for the freedom of Neverland. The sad parallels, however, went far beyond fiction. Many of the children that took part in the Pedro Pan exodus never saw their parents again. Mothers and fathers remained trapped on the island, denied exit visas by an increasingly capricious, and vindictive, Castro. Most of the children never saw their homeland again.

Most, though, went on to lead productive, even successful, lives in their new land. Their ranks include judges and journalists, singers, and at least one U.S. senator. Among them, too, was Miguel Bezos, the stepfather of Amazon founder and *Washington Post* owner Jeff Bezos.

It had not been my intention to divide families. I am sorry for those who were hurt. My goal had been only to deepen the discontent with the government, to sow more instability, and, hopefully, to create the conditions for its downfall. I succeeded in the first two; I failed in the last.

CONSPIRACIES, INTELLIGENCE GATHERING, spying, sabotage, infiltration, and all the other aspects of what I was taught have existed since time immemorial. So, too, political assassinations. Medieval kings and queens sent their agents into the courts of their enemies, and their friends, to spy, to learn of plots and battle plans. Enemies were poisoned, kidnapped, lured into ambushes, or had their throats slit in the night by a lover.

Methods had changed, become more advanced, but the underlying principles and goals remained the same. Machiavelli had first described it: the ends justify the means. And I knew that there was nothing that we would do against him that Castro had not, and would not, do against his enemies. Against us.

He already had. Castro knew not to make the mistake that Batista had. He knew that if the opposition was allowed to grow, it could become unstoppable. He knew that if he showed his enemies the same kind of mercy that Batista had shown him when he released Castro from prison, he could face a similar result. He also knew that the United States saw him as a threat, and while the yanquis might not be prepared to risk the public outcry that would surely follow if they sent their armies to remove him, that hardly meant they would stand idly by while he consolidated his power. Fidel was well aware that the colossus to the north supported his enemies. He knew the U.S.

government was training and supplying people like me. He knew that while the war was not officially declared, it was still a war.

So Castro took advice and training from the Soviets. He learned their KGB tactics and used them against his people. The repression didn't come all at once. It came in slowly, like the rising tide, until all Cuba was drowning. But even in those early days, I could see it coming.

Soon enough, the surveillance network of undercover agents and informers would grow and began summarily detaining—often for extended periods—anyone even suspected of opposing him. Labor "unions" would begin reporting on the loyalty of their members, and those found to be questionable would be removed. A climate of fear would spread across the island until no one dared trust anyone, even members of their own family. With enough fear would come paralysis. People wouldn't dare to resist.

But not yet.

Not all of us, anyway.

MELTON AND BISHOP contended that the fundamental purpose of a clandestine operative was to cause psychological or economic sabotage. Sometimes, that required bombs.

By the time Pedro Pan began, the reports of sabotage and attacks had become common. They came by ground, on the water, from the air.

The Cuban government documented the first aerial bombing assault of 1960 when the year was barely twelve days old. According to the state-run Center for American Studies, a plane dropped incendiary bombs in the areas of Bainoa, Caraballo, and San Antonio de Río Blanco. Another made a similar assault on cane fields adjacent to the Hershey factory about thirty miles east of Havana.

More followed. The center reported air attacks against cane fields in Güines, Las Villas, Cojímar, and Regla, at five locations in Camagüey and three more in Oriente, another in Matanzas, and at the Central Toledo in Havana. In January alone.

The attacks continued in February, destroying more than ten million pounds of sugar cane. Fires set by clandestine members of the resistance on the ground caused the loss of another ten million pounds of cane the following month.

By the end of the year, the fight moved into the cities. Warehouses, factories, and department stores became the targets of counterrevolutionary fighters. I was one of them.

I abandoned the propaganda tactics Bishop had taught me in favor of more direct, and violent, means. I was never what we in Cuba call a "man of action." Not direct action, anyway. I remained behind the scenes, using my administrative skills to organize and plan these violent disruptions. I built small cells of resistance fighters and discovered a talent for strategizing I never knew I had.

I became a terrorist.

Using the skills Bishop and Melton taught me, I became the chief of sabotage for the newly formed Movimiento Revolucionario del Pueblo (the People's Revolutionary Movement, known by its initials, MRP). The CIA supplied us with plastic explosives and other incendiary materials. I used them to launch bombing attacks against a series of urban targets. The goal now was to spread fear, and cause irrevocable economic damage.

I was hardly alone.

In December, bombs went off at the Cantabria bar, in the America Theater, and in the cafeteria of the Flogar department store in mid-Havana, injuring fifteen people.

On New Year's Eve, an arson fire at La Época, one of Havana's biggest and best-known department stores, set a blaze that took firefighters twenty-two hours to put out. Damage was estimated at more than ten million pesos.

On January 8, fire destroyed a mattress store in downtown Havana. Six days later, the Rothschild Samuell Duiga tobacco warehouse was set ablaze, causing 3.4 million pesos in damage. The following month, a white phosphorus device went off at the El Encanto department store in Santiago, causing extensive fire damage. A week later, a car bomb exploded in the garage of the Hotel Habana Libre, and two days after that an explosive device destroyed a fuel tanker-truck and damaged five more vehicles at the Belot oil refinery in the Port of Havana. One of our bombs at the central aqueduct knocked out water throughout most of the capital for two full days. Two explosions caused nearly one and a half million pesos' worth of damage at a pair of Woolworth's in the capital.

I was the organizer. The strategist. The brain. But I didn't plant the bombs. I couldn't. I couldn't run the risk of being caught. I knew all the secrets.

I relied heavily on what are known as *petacas incendiarias*, easily concealed firebombs packed the size of a cigarette pack or a hip flask. Armed with a time-delayed fuse, they could be smuggled into a building and hidden inside without attracting attention and spread fierce, hard-to-extinguish flames when they detonated hours later.

I made them, I set them, and I gave them to my people. And I told them, don't forget to try to put it in a place where there won't be any dead. In a garbage can. Late at night. In a parked car.

One of my devices was discovered before it went off at Fin de Siglo, and state security agents surprised and arrested one of our members as she placed one of the *petacas* at Sears. Several members of the group worried that she might talk.

"You know," one of them said to me, "she knows everybody in the group. If they get it out of her, we all get to make the firing squad."

I don't know what the authorities did to her. I don't know how they might have tried to make her talk. Apparently, she did. A month after she was arrested, Cuban security rushed in one morning and arrested seven more members of the MRP.

The final and most devastating of the firebombings I coordinated came on April 13, 1960. El Encanto was the Manhattan Macy's of Cuba, the most important store in the country. The fire there shook the regime to its very foundations. El Encanto stood in the very heart of Havana's retail district, on a street lined with shops, boutiques, and novelty stores, just steps from the La Moda furrier and the Casa Quintana jewelry store.

One of our MRP members, Carlos González Vidal, worked as a salesman in the records department on the second floor. He lingered a while after the store closed and made his way to the fabrics department. Once he found himself alone, he pulled out the small incendiary device loaded with C-4 explosive that I had prepared for him. His instructions were simple, and he carried them out perfectly. The timer was already set. He slipped the device between two rolls of fabric and left. The placement was crucial. Not only would the cloth conceal the device, it would also provide fuel when the powerful plastique detonated and ignited everything in close proximity.

Carlos stepped into a waiting car two blocks from the store, and by the time the blast sparked the initial blaze at close to 7:00 p.m., he was nearly twenty miles away at a safe house in Playa Baracoa, waiting for the boat that would take him to the United States.

The blast went according to plan, except for one thing. The fire that followed spread quickly, feeding off the bolts of fabric, growing in intensity as it raced through the department, shot through the air conditioning ducts into other sections and onto other floors, and began consuming the seven-story structure from the inside. Within an hour, the interior walls begin to collapse. Giant tongues of flame burst through the windows and licked at the sky.

Firefighters and volunteers surrounded the building, pouring tons of water on the blaze. They fought hour after hour through the night but could do little more than hope to keep the fire from spreading to neighboring stores packed tightly on the block.

The sun came up and still they fought. Then, somewhere during the heat of the day, the building groaned and gave way. It collapsed in a thundering mass of ash and rubble, sending a great column of smoke up toward the sky. And still it burned.

The fire that began with a single *petaca* raged for twenty-two hours before it finally died. When it was over, only the scarred skeleton of what had once been Cuba's most significant store remained.

Then the horrible tragedy we had tried so carefully to avoid came to light. The blast had been timed to go off after the store had emptied, when all the customers and every employee were gone for the day. But in an effort to thwart the rash of arsons and bombings that proved the existence of a strong resistance movement, the government had begun placing militia members as security guards to stand watch. One sentry, a forty-three-year-old mother of two named Fe del Valle Ramos, was trapped inside as the inferno sped through the building.

Firemen sifted through the debris for nearly two days before they found her charred remains. The authorities found Carlos much sooner. The lights playing out from the house on the beach where he had fled, and the flurry of late-night activity, aroused their suspicion.

He didn't crumble during the interrogation. Instead, he proudly took responsibility for the destruction and defiantly proclaimed it a blow for freedom in the name of the counterrevolution. He went valiantly to his death, shouting, "Long live free Cuba," just before the roar of the firing squad silenced him forever. He was twenty-one.

The revolution turned Fe del Valle into a heroic martyr who died at the hands of terrorists while bravely doing her duty for her country.

Four days later, the entire nation's attention turned elsewhere. The long-anticipated U.S.-backed invasion had finally begun. Everyone knew it was coming. Even Castro. The only surprise was where and when.

On April 17, all of Cuba learned both.

I was as surprised as anyone when the brigade of CIA-trained Cuban exiles came crashing ashore at the Bay of Pigs. The CIA had kept all of its operatives and counterrevolutionary contacts as much in the dark as everyone else. The excuse they gave us, later, was that there were too many groups, with too many tongues. With so many organizations, they said, they knew Castro had to have infiltrated some. They just didn't know which ones. So they didn't tell anyone.

That was their excuse. But I had already come to realize that their conception of Cubans in general was that we talked too much and that we liked intrigue. Melton and Bishop both made that clear.

They told me that I couldn't involve anyone else in my activities unless I had absolute confidence in them. The risk was too great. I had to know them. I had to trust them. Even then, I should keep my contacts to a small circle. I shouldn't involve too many people. More people meant more mouths, and more chance that someone in the group would talk. Either because they were with the government, because they slipped, or because they just had big mouths and big egos and wanted the world to know they were big men.

They were right. A lot of people ended up in prison in Cuba because of that.

I was once invited to a meeting of counterrevolutionaries who wanted me to help them with a plot they were hatching. A couple of them knew me and invited me to come along. I knew them, so I went. But when I got to the house, there must have been twenty people inside. Bishop and Melton had already taught me to steer clear of big groups in general, and to avoid gatherings of big groups like the plague.

I listened. I never organized a cell that had more than five people in it, including me. It was safer. For me, and them. They were connected to me, but not to one another. It was like a firewall. I knew that members of separate cells that both worked with me could come together and never know they both knew me. And none of them knew I worked with the CIA.

So when I showed up at the meeting and saw enough people to fill a party bus, I turned around and left. I never stepped inside. I looked past the person who opened the door, saw the packed room, and immediately started backing away before anyone inside could see me. I acted like I'd knocked on the wrong door.

"Oh, my god!" I said. "I'm so stupid. This isn't the fourth floor. It's the third. Please forgive me. I'm sorry to have bothered you."

I was gone before he even finished telling me it was all right, "anybody can make a mistake."

The next day I heard that the police had raided the meeting and arrested everyone. Someone inside was with the government, or told somebody who was.

Fidel was good at that kind of thing, infiltrating movements, even before taking over the government. Even back when he was opposing Batista, he would infiltrate people into other opposition movements, so that he could know what his "allies" were up to. It was a small step for him to turn the same kind of tactics against the people of Cuba after he became prime minister.

So I understood the CIA's caution. But they were wrong about so many things concerning the Bay of Pigs.

Agency officials told Kennedy that the people would rise up once the invasion began. That wasn't true. It wasn't close to true. The Pentagon knew it wasn't. They told the president that. They didn't expect the Cubans to do anything. Not even the ones the CIA had been supplying with weapons. And there were a lot of those.

The CIA encouraged, trained, and financed the best of the Cuban youth that opposed Communism. And they made sure they had what they needed for terrorism. They supplied C3 and C-4 military explosives. They provided them with M3 fully automatic machine guns. They provided the incendiary *petacas* that facilitated spectacular acts of sabotage against businesses, industries, and important state property.

The CIA delivered tons of weapons. A savage number of weapons. They dropped them offshore, just threw them in the water in special sealed bags. Our boats would go out later and retrieve them from the bottom of the sea. Then they'd unload them at different places around the island. One of the places where I picked up ours was at the Club Náutico, right in Havana—right under the government's nose.

When we had to move them, we put them in burlap bags. Big, heavy ones. We'd put something else in the bag with them, a chair or something, so it would disguise the shape. We'd also put a pillow or something in, too, so the weapons didn't clatter too much and attract attention. Then we'd just carry them out and put them in the trunks of our cars.

It was always best, Bishop taught me, to do it somewhere in the middle of the day. Not at night. At night it seems more suspicious, like you're sneaking around. People ask questions. It seems more natural in broad daylight, when there are lots of people out and about. Then no one would imagine what you're really doing. I mean, who would transport weapons when there's a crowd around? That would be crazy, right?

I remember one shipment that just seemed obscenely large: incendiary bombs, smoke bombs, *petacas*, C3, C-4, a machine gun, hand guns, and ammunition. There was enough for fifty men. Easily.

Of course, it didn't always go well.

The first weapons drop was a disaster. As writer Evan Thomas described it, the CIA made its first attempt on September 28, 1960.

An airplane carrying enough weapons for one hundred men tried making a drop to an agent waiting on the ground. "The air crew missed the drop zone by seven miles and landed the weapons on top of a dam, where Castro's forces scooped them up. The agent was caught and shot."

Maybe that's why they turned to boats.

But the CIA still overestimated what we were capable of doing once the Bay of Pigs invasion actually began. It's one thing to burn a store, but to arm and activate a grassroots army and help take over a country . . . that's a different challenge.

Even if any of the opposition groups had considered joining forces with the Bay of Pigs invaders, they couldn't. The moment the troops started rushing the shore at Playa Girón, Cuban security forces started rounding up everyone connected to the opposition. They took them to the giant sports stadium east of Havana and held them there, under arrest, until well after the invasion had been repelled and the attackers mopped up.

The invasion itself was a fiasco. The preparations were shoddy. The CIA-trained exile fighters were outnumbered and outgunned. Then they were cut loose, left to fight until their ammunition was gone, with no support and no chance to retreat. There was nowhere for them to go.

Twelve hundred men landed. Castro had two hundred thousand. The CIA knew that beforehand. The CIA was well aware that the twelve hundred idealistic Cuban exiles thrown against the heavily defended remote beachhead couldn't win. Nor did the agency believe that the invasion would spark a successful uprising. What CIA Director Allen Dulles was counting on was his ability to pressure young President John F. Kennedy into launching an all-out U.S. military invasion of the island after the Bay of Pigs brigade got bogged down on the beaches. But Kennedy shocked Dulles and the other gray-haired military and intelligence advisors by refusing to buckle. JFK had told them all along that he didn't want a "noisy" invasion, and he refused to expand the CIA operation into an all-out war, even if it meant sacrificing the brave *brigadistas*.

The new president had inherited the CIA's duplicitous invasion plan from the Eisenhower administration. Now he was blamed for its failure. It earned him the hatred of Cubans and the CIA alike.

It also earned him Che Guevara's mocking praise. In August, El Che sent Kennedy a note. "Thanks for Playa Girón," he wrote. "Before the invasion, the revolution was weak. Now it's stronger than ever."

Kennedy, of course, blamed the CIA. He felt, correctly, that he had been lied to. The agency advisors had given him the information they wanted him to have, not a true analysis, and certainly not the facts he needed to make an appropriate assessment to base his decisions on. He felt betrayed. In response, JFK vowed to tear apart the CIA. He began by forcing Dulles, the agency's legendary spymaster, to resign, along with his two top deputies and others.

That only made Kennedy's enemies in the CIA hate him even more. And I don't think that they made much of an effort to hide it.

I had never heard Bishop speak negatively about the president before the invasion. The next time I saw him, the month after I had left Cuba for Miami, his bitterness came through at the mere mention of the president's name, or of the Bay of Pigs.

He blamed the "immature" and "inexperienced" Kennedy—a "political adolescent"—for the "debacle."

His disdain for the president extended to the entire Kennedy clan. He disparaged them repeatedly. "Those good-looking boys have forgotten their dark roots," he'd say. "But the apple doesn't fall far from the tree. John Kennedy's grandfather was an Irish terrorist. His father made his fortune with Scotch whiskey during Prohibition. It's easy to be a liberal when your belly's full. It's hard to do the right thing when the wrong thing is in your blood."

Following the failed invasion, his anger boiled over. He sent me a message dripping with disgust. He understood the consequences of the failure, but he needed more information so he could "piece together the puzzle" that would explain the "humiliating defeat." He asked me to survey the scene of the battle and give him a report on what had occurred.

The site had been declared off-limits to anyone without official permission. I took a chance and got a friend to get me what I needed. It didn't take me long to recognize that the expedition never had a chance. My report to Bishop was short: "They were outnumbered 100 to 1. Castro's forces had better weapons and more of them."

IN HIS BOOK, Phillips recalled his deeply emotional reaction as it became clear the invasion was collapsing. After he finally left the operations center at Quarters Eye in Washington, D.C., and went home, he got drunk in his backyard listening to news reports about Cuba on a portable radio:

> Suddenly my stomach churned. I was sick. My body heaved.
> Then I began to cry.
> I wept for two hours. I was sick again, then drunk again. . . .
> Oh shit! Shit!

In our final conversation over lunch before Bishop left for the United States, back in March 1960, he had mused that the situation in Cuba had a simple solution.

"I have this theory," he said, "that if Fidel died, the revolution would be over."

At the moment, at least, he didn't seem to be suggesting that I do it. Just that that's what would happen.

"Yes," he continued, as if ruminating out loud. "It all revolves around him. The best way for this to end is for Fidel Castro to die."

In fact, CIA plans for Castro's assassination were set in motion that year, while President Eisenhower was still in office. That September, CIA contractor Robert Maheu met with Mafia emissary Johnny Rosselli in New York City, offering him $150,000 for the "removal" of Castro. After the Bay of Pigs, the agency escalated its efforts against Castro. I received a terse message from Bishop printed in invisible ink. He told me that Bernardo Corrales had what I needed to give Cuba its simple solution.

He meant, of course, that I should begin putting together my own plan to assassinate Castro. We would refer to it as Operation Liborio.

"Liborio" is a symbol of national pride in Cuba, like Uncle Sam in the United States. Unlike the U.S. mascot, though, Liborio doesn't represent the government. He represents the people. Liborio is depicted as a humble and put-upon farmer with a self-deprecating sense of humor and a long dark beard, whose droll observations on politics and politicians make him a voice for the hoi polloi.

By handing me the high-stakes Operation Liborio assignment, Bishop was making a statement. My time had come. With that message, he was telling me that I had graduated. I had already gone from being a simple accountant to a counterrevolutionary leading a propaganda campaign, and then to a bomb maker and terrorist. Now he was saying I could be even more, that I could be someone who could change the course of history.

Before I could make this leap, though, I had one more thing to do. I had to send my family to safety. I had to get them off the island to a new life, not knowing if I would ever see them again.

In the summer of 1961, I took my wife by the hand.

"Sira, my love," I said. "You and the kids must leave. I have things I must do, missions I must complete."

She knew, of course, that I was working aggressively against Castro. She didn't know the details, but she knew.

"I don't want any harm to come to our children," I continued. "I know you don't, either. If you're all here, it's very possible that they could try to use you to catch me. It's better if you leave."

She was very strong. She didn't cry. She didn't argue. All she said was, "Will I see you again?"

I hesitated. I didn't really have an answer. She was strong. She was also very religious.

"I'm in God's hands," I said.

I sent them to Spain, to Madrid, then Barcelona. Cubans could still travel in those days, but not freely. I had to buy them round-trip tickets so that they would appear to be returning. They could take nothing with them, except for a few items of clothes and enough cash for a vacation. The children didn't know they'd be staying in Spain until after they got there. Tony, the oldest of the three, was five.

Then I went underground.

The government was already clamping down by that point. In February, the Cuban army captured Lino Fernández and five hundred of his men who had taken up arms in Santa Clara. In March, two of Castro's former military aides, Major Jesús Carreras Zayas and Major William A. Morgan, an American who had led a column of rebels against Batista, were charged with treason and executed. A week later, Humberto Sorí Marín, Fidel's former agriculture minister and his chief judge at the 1959 war crimes trials, was arrested for conspiring against the government. He was executed the following month.

After the Bay of Pigs, it got worse. By the end of April it was estimated that twenty thousand Cubans had been arrested, suspected of "counterrevolutionary activities."

I wasn't being followed, but I wasn't taking chances. I went undercover. I left my house. I had an apartment in the Vedado, the Havana business district, that I used, but I only went there to sleep. And not always. I moved around a lot, to different safe houses. I never spent more than three or four nights in the same place.

I went out as little as possible. When I did, I watched to see if I was being followed. Bishop and Melton had taught me what to look for. If you're really being followed, they said, it's never just one car. That's how they trick you. They use two. One follows you for a little bit, then turns. Everything seems normal. When you see it turn, you think, "Oh, I was wrong. They weren't following me, after all." You breathe easy. You don't even notice the other car, turning at the corner and falling in behind you a couple of cars back.

I only met with one or two people at a time. We'd arrive separately. We'd park our cars at a distance so there wouldn't be a bunch of cars in front of the place. If we were supposed to meet at seven, one would arrive at 6:05, another at 6:20 or 6:25. Sometimes I'd get there last. Sometimes I'd get there first, and be waiting, so I could be sure the others came alone.

Nobody knew my real name. They knew me only as Víctor.

As soon as it started getting dark, I'd head inside. I spent a lot of time alone. I spent a lot of time reading. I read one book, Orwell's *Animal Farm*, again and again. It reminded me of Cuba.

Then, in October, the plan I had been working on failed. My simple solution to the Cuba situation, ending Fidel's reign with a bazooka in the night, failed. I left, according to plan.

It was the end of my days in Cuba, but not the end of my fight against Fidel—or my attempts to assassinate him.

chapter 7
ALPHA 66 AND A MAN NAMED LEE

THE MONTH AFTER I got to Miami, I heard from Bishop. He wasn't done with Cuba, or Kennedy.

We met on a street corner downtown and walked a while, talking. The failed assassination attempt in Havana was disappointing, to both of us. He said it looked like the fight against Fidel was going to take longer than either of us had expected, or hoped. He had some ideas about what we should do, he said.

"You know you can count on me," I said.

"Good," he said. "It's important for us to know we can count on each other. And trust each other."

"I agree," I said. "I think I've always shown you that you can trust me. And I always will."

Bishop stopped.

"Really?" he asked. "Will you? Right now?"

"How do you mean?"

"Will you sign a contract saying that? Right now?"

Pedestrians flowed past us on the sidewalk.

"Here?" I asked.

"No," he said, nodding up the street. "Just up ahead."

He led me to the Pan American Bank Building. We took the elevator up, then he pulled out a key and opened one of the doors in the hall. The door was bare, with no number or sign indicating what type of business might be on the other side. He closed it behind us and asked me to wait a moment, then disappeared through another door inside. He came back with two men, holding several papers.

"Read these and sign them, please," Bishop said.

The other men stood stiffly as I looked the papers over. They seemed to be contracts, and some kind of formal pledge.

As I later told journalist and congressional investigator Gaeton Fonzi, "It was a pledge of my loyalty, a secret pledge. I think they wanted to impress on me my responsibility and my commitment to the cause."

After I finished signing, Bishop thanked the two men and led me out of the office. "Now we can talk," he said. "Let me tell you what I have in mind."

He was direct, as always. He wanted me to start a paramilitary group, composed of exiles, to carry out attacks against Cuba. He made it clear that he had no respect for the Castro opposition group supported by President Kennedy.

"The Cuban Revolutionary Council is a joke," he said. "They just do what Kennedy tells them to. You need to form a group that will really do something. That will take action."

"With men of action," I said.

"Yes," he said. "And, Tony, just remember, these operations, everything you do, can never connect to us. They are the actions of independent anti-Castro Cuban exiles, acting totally on their own."

He smiled.

"But if you need any help, let me know."

He didn't mean money. That was still our own responsibility. And he didn't mean he could completely clear the way for us to do as we pleased. But just as in Cuba, he could help us get weapons. And even more than in Cuba, he could help us with information. The rest of the rules remained the way they were when I was back on the island. No one could ever know I was working with the CIA.

I went to Puerto Rico, where a number of CPAs I had known in Havana were now living. They had formed a new accounting association, made up of exiles. I knew they had money and, importantly, connections to powerful and wealthy exile businessmen who would be willing to give money and assistance to the fight against Castro. Plus, they knew me.

The word went out through the exile community. The group that showed up for our first meeting included much more than accountants. Exiles from all walks of life showed up. They must have been waiting for someone like me to step forward, to offer them a chance to take part. I had been in Puerto Rico less than two weeks and already I counted sixty-five people in the room, besides me.

"I didn't come here to resume my profession," I told them. "I came here to resume the fight."

I looked around the room. I saw many faces that were new to me. Most, in fact.

"I was an accountant in Cuba. I worked for Julio Lobo," I said. "I was also a counterrevolutionary. Some of you here know me. You know that El Encanto no longer exists because of me."

A murmur ran through the room.

"But I was once like all of you," I continued, "wanting to stop what was happening in Cuba, wanting to see my homeland—our homeland—free, and not knowing what to do."

I looked out at the expectant faces before me.

"Now I do. This is the beginning," I said. "We are the beginning. Of Castro's end."

They began to applaud, but I wasn't done. I remembered my Catholic lessons, of the Greek letters symbolizing eternal salvation, A and Ω, the beginning and end.

"We are Alpha," I said. Then, quickly adding myself to the number in the room, I continued, "We are Alpha 66—the beginning of the end for Castro!"

Their applause thundered. It shook the walls.

Winning the accountants' support proved to be easy. They gave money of their own and quickly went out and raised more. Our bank account—our war chest—swelled. El Che would have been proud—from each according to his abilities, they gave. They helped organize, recruit members, schedule meetings. And we grew.

But these were men like me. Planners. Administrators. We were good at building an organization, but we were not "men of action." For that, I needed to look elsewhere, in the largest Cuban exile community of them all.

I went back to Miami, where Sira and the kids awaited. They had left Spain shortly after I left Cuba. I had sent my parents into exile with them. Now that I had arrived safely, accompanied by my mother-in-law, the family reunited.

Tony and Ana were old enough to go to school, beginning classes in English for the first time. Sira found a job at a shoe factory.

"You have other work to do," she said.

I was dedicated to Alpha, and turning it into more than a name. We needed brave men, fighting men, who knew weapons and how to use them, and were willing to risk their lives.

Finding the resources I needed among the Miami exiles, though, proved difficult. Both money and men were committed to the Revolutionary Council, or to other anti-Castro groups that had begun to sprout up. To most, I was merely an accountant with his hand out, talking about forming yet another group.

That changed, thanks to a friend. He introduced me to one of the bravest men I have ever known, a simple, soft-spoken man who let his actions speak more loudly than any words ever could. And, like me, he was a man finding a less-than-welcome reception in Miami.

Eloy Gutiérrez Menoyo had taken up arms against Batista in Cuba and wound up leading an army. It was, as Bishop said disparagingly about the Kennedys, in his blood. Only his veins, Bishop had to admit, boiled with a fierce Spaniard's blood.

Menoyo's oldest brother died fighting the Fascists in Spain's civil war. After the family moved to Cuba, another brother died fighting Batista. Menoyo took his place. Fidel built his stronghold in the Sierra Maestra mountains far from Havana in Cuba's east. Menoyo built an army nearly as large as Castro's in the Escambray, in the island's center, leading an independent guerrilla battle until finally joining with Castro in the final days of the war.

He could be seen famously marching alongside Castro in Havana after Batista had fled. But he was never a part of Castro's government; alarmed by the signs of Fidel's growing dictatorship, he fled Cuba in a boat with eleven supporters at the start of 1961.

Menoyo didn't take part in the Bay of Pigs. But he was determined to overthrow Castro. Because of his earlier ties to the revolution, however, he found few to help him in Miami.

They didn't trust him, or they didn't like him. Neither did Bishop. I did, as soon as I met him. I found him to be quietly confident, unassuming, and refreshingly sincere. He had deep convictions and was dedicated to his cause. He was also a staunch leftist who believed firmly in socialist ideals. He was not, however, a Communist. That, to him, was just a form of authoritarian rule, a system that stole the freedom of the very people it purported to liberate.

All that was a fine point of distinction that was lost in the fervor of exile politics. But not on me. I was taken with his honesty and I knew his capacity. Eloy had already seen more battle in a quarter century of life than most of the big-talking exiles ever would. When I met him, he was twenty-seven years old.

I was not mistaken. He always did exactly what he said he would do. Menoyo's vision was clear. He was determined to lead a landing force in Cuba and head once again into the Escambray to build another guerrilla army and to topple Fidel.

He needed money and weapons, and enough capable men to form its core.

"Together," I said, "we can do that. I know how to get money and weapons. Together, we'll get the men."

Eloy Menoyo became Alpha 66's military chief. I became its face.

I spent half my time in Miami and half my time in Puerto Rico. Generally, two weeks at a time. I also traveled around the country—Chicago, Texas, L.A. I went to places where Cubans like me were making livings and making lives, but always—always!—dreaming of the day they would return. So they joined. And they gave. And they pointed me to others who would, too.

By July, we had $64,000 in cash on hand, and more coming in.

Bishop was pleased with my progress, but cautious about Menoyo. He had thought more about our tactics, he said, and now knew exactly what we should do.

The CIA's plan, via Maurice Bishop, had always been to put the fight on Kennedy's doorstep, to force him to take the offensive to end Cuba's Communist government.

World events were helping. By the middle of 1962, it was no secret to the CIA that the Soviets were giving Castro military support. Soviet troops disguised as technicians were flooding the island. Despite the precautions taken by the Soviets and the Cuban authorities, the anti-Castro underground was the first to divulge details of what was happening.

The United States grew increasingly worried about what appeared to be a looming confrontation with the Soviet Union over Cuba. And that played right into Bishop's hand. The best way to avoid a fight with the Soviets, he said, would be to take Cuba out of the picture.

"If Castro goes," he said, "Communism goes. And so do the Soviets. If Kennedy wants to avoid a war with Khrushchev, he'll have to make one with Fidel."

That's where Alpha 66 came in, he said. But not with guerrilla warfare. With a new hit-and-run approach. That, Bishop believed, would bring quicker results.

"You don't hit Castro directly," he said. "You hit him where it hurts. You hit ships bringing goods to Cuba."

"Cuban ships?" I asked.

"Yes," he said. "But not just Cuban ships. Any ships. Merchant ships. Russian ships. Ships from the Soviet bloc. If they do business with Cuba, they're targets."

"And then?" I asked.

"When the Soviets start complaining and rattling their sabers, Kennedy has to act," he said.

"What if he doesn't take aim at Cuba?" I asked. "What if he takes aim at the CIA?"

"That's exactly why we have Alpha 66. When they accuse us, we'll tell him that we had nothing to do with it. It's a bunch of anti-Castro exiles acting on their own."

I didn't know the term then, but he was talking about something that subsequently turned out to be an all-too-common practice for the agency, "plausible deniability." It also sounded extremely similar to the kind of thinking that had led to the Bay of Pigs disaster.

I didn't say that to Bishop. Instead I said, "Alpha already has other plans in motion. Menoyo is our military chief. He believes we should infiltrate Cuba with a group of men and start a guerilla war."

I could see Bishop tensing.

"Menoyo has a lot of faith in his plan," I said. "He's already sent word to some of his contacts in the internal resistance on the island. You're talking about a complete change of direction. That would be a tremendous obstacle for his plans."

Bishop jabbed a finger at me.

"Please, Tony," he said, "don't cause problems. He listens to you. Explain to him that an Army may march on its belly, but Alpha 66 needs cash. And so does he if he wants to be able to fight in the mountains for any length of time."

"We're already raising money," I said.

"Yes. And well. But imagine what would happen after people saw Alpha 66 actually taking action. Not just talking about it. High-profile attacks on Soviet ships will be a fund-raising bonanza.

"Tell him," Bishop continued, "that holding off on his plans now will only help them in the future."

Said, and done. I met with Eloy and told him I thought delaying his plans would be better. I never mentioned Bishop, or the CIA. Not to him, or anyone. Ever. I let him think it was my idea. He bought it. I'll never forget his ironic smile.

"That makes sense," he said. "But I wonder about the consequences of attacking their ships. It may do more harm than good."

I started to open my mouth to protest. He stopped me.

"We need money to buy bullets and boots," he said. "Not to mention food."

WE WENT TO work. We bought boats. We bought guns. We set up bases in the Bahamas, first at Anguilla, then Andros Island. They were remote and sparsely inhabited.

"There's more goats than people on Andros," Eloy once said.

They were also tantalizingly close to Cuba.

Our first attack came in September 1962, against a merchant ship anchored in a Cuban port. By mistake, the ship was British. We made the most of it, anyway.

A *Newsweek* article later described it:

Just after 2:00 a.m., the small unmarked craft, a former American PT boat, swerved in near the Cuban port of Caibarien. It fired a few volleys of machine gun fire at two Cuban ships and a British freighter, then fled. Thus, a month ago, Alpha 66 made its first strike against Castro.

Back at headquarters in San Juan, Puerto Rico, Antonio Veciana, the spokesman for Alpha 66, had only one complaint: He had budgeted the raid at $3,600, but it cost $5,823.

The FBI had known the attack was coming, and that more were soon to follow. The CIA told them. "The following information concerning Alpha 66, a Cuban counterrevolutionary group, was received on 7 September 1962," an interagency memo from the CIA's deputy director (plans) began.

"It is dedicated to sabotage, harassment and similar hit and run type commando operations against the Castro regime in Cuba," it continued, "and intends to carry out six to eight such forrays [sic] in the coming months. The first of these is reportedly already planned in detail and will go into effect in the not too distant future, stemming from some undisclosed island base in the Caribbean."

The memo added that we had "enough supplies to carry out their first operation successfully and maybe one other," along with about $30,000 remaining in various bank accounts. It went on to describe some of our fund-raising efforts and noted: "As ex-CPA's their very businesslike manner requires them to give receipts for any funds received for help."

The CIA fanned the flames even more three days later. "SUBJECT: POSSIBLE IMMINENT STRIKE AT HABANA, CUBA BY ALPHA 66 ORGANIZATION," the flash message began. Its recipients included officials in the FBI, the State Department, and the Defense Intelligence Agency, as well as the Army, Navy, and Air Force. The message revealed that the attack was scheduled for 2:00 a.m. on September 10 or 11, and it mentioned me by name: "Veciana has had no sleep during the past 48 hours due to his listening for news and making contacts in preparation for future operations."

Much more important, the agency message revealed some of the depth of the CIA's information about the operation. It said the crew consisted of five men, with at least one "Anti-tank type" weapon, and that the boat was hiding among the keys near Cuba.

A separate teletype added "two fifty caliber machine guns" to the armaments.

"The original plan for the strike . . . included the boat captain's suggestion that an American flag be flown by the boat . . ." it continued. "But Veciana vetoed this with words 'Not Yet'. . ."

WE WEREN'T ALONE. I don't know how many other groups were working with the CIA or on their own, but the armed fight against Castro involved many actors. They were stopped by the U.S. Coast Guard setting out from the Florida Keys, or caught loading weapons onto boats. They issued press statements contending they'd been fired upon by Cuban forces, and offered breathtaking accounts of their exploits.

The Directorio Revolucionario Estudiantil (DRE), Revolutionary Student Directorate, carried out what they described as a commando attack on a hotel and theater in the beachfront Miramar section of

Havana, blasting the buildings with a 20 mm cannon from a boat two hundred yards offshore.

One of the boat's gas tanks began to leak just as they "got close enough for the raiders to see the lights of Cuba," the Associated Press reported. "We didn't know what to do," said the gunner, a "young, slender" José Basulto. "The gas was right under the cannon, and I was going to shoot it. We were afraid the shots might spark and cause an explosion.

"But there was Cuba . . ." he said.

Basulto, who would later go on to found Brothers to the Rescue, an exile group dedicated to aiding Cuban rafters spotted on the dangerous trek across the Florida Straits, didn't hesitate: "When the word came, I opened up on the hotel dining room, where Castro was supposed to be holding the meeting with the Russians. We could only hope he was there, too," he said. "I must have shot about twenty-six times. It was really something. I could see the shells break into the hotel windows, and then all the lights went out."

I don't know if Bishop worked with the DRE as well. But the announcement they released had all the earmarks of his strategy. The purpose of the raid, it said, was to "denounce the arrival of increasingly large contingents of Russian troops to our island."

And, with words that sounded as if they were coming straight from Bishop's mouth, the DRE challenged President Kennedy to remember his promise "that Cuba would never be abandoned."

"We will not tolerate peaceful coexistence," the DRE statement continued. "We are not concerned with interested groups or long-range tactics of large powers. We are concerned only that over the tombs of Martí and Maceo they do not raise the soiled banners of the hammer and sickle."

In Bishop's view, putting pressure on the Soviets was justifiable. But once again, he didn't anticipate Kennedy's obstinacy. We continued with our plan to attack Soviet merchant ships in Cuban ports. And with making sure the world, and Kennedy, would know.

Alpha 66 made the news again a month after our first raid, this time under the dramatic headline: "We'll Hit All Ships to Cuba, Alpha 66 Threatens."

"Cuban exile commandos declared 'war' today on all shipping to Cuba and boldly announced that raids like that in which 20 Russians and Cuban militia were killed this week will be repeated," read the opening to the October 11, 1962, *Miami News* story.

Then the newspaper account paraphrased me, saying I vowed that Alpha 66 "fighters will attack any and all vessels taking supplies to Castro—not just those from Iron Curtain countries."

The article reminded readers of the September attack, then added, "Veciana, a certified public accountant, said his force of 30 men killed 'no fewer' than 20 Russians and Cubans in a raid on a Cuban north coast fishing village Monday night. He said the commandos suffered five casualties but declined to say if any were killed."

I said it. But it never happened.

Bishop had told me to embellish, exaggerate, outright lie if I wanted to, all for the sake of making our belligerence seem more capable, and more threatening. I agreed because, let's face it, a boat with three or four guys shooting at the side of a massive iron ship—what could that possibly do?

One objective was to let the Soviets know that we weren't happy about them making a continued military and economic investment in Cuba. The other was to force Kennedy to stop ignoring the Cuban situation. So we inflated our numbers, aggrandized our accomplishments, and reported losses to keep things from seeming too one-sided.

An Associated Press story dated October 30 carried the headline: "2 Alpha 66 Boats Lost on Cuba strike." Followed by: "Alpha 66, militant anti-Castro band, today reported that two of its vessels on a mission to attack a military objective in Cuba sank in heavy seas last week. . . . All 11 members of the expedition escaped, it was reported."

No one questioned the timing of the reported attack, nor how it would have been possible for a group of exile commandos to thread their way through waters filled with U.S. and Soviet naval ships, pierce an ironclad naval blockade, and slip, sight unseen, toward Cuba. Nor did they wonder how we could have then foundered in the "heavy seas," radioed for help, and had more of our paramilitary craft—PT boats, mind you—get through the same barriers to pick us up and carry us back home, with neither them nor our radio communications attracting attention.

Because, at that very moment, Cuba had just brought the world to the brink of disaster.

A week before the story about our boats appeared, John Kennedy went on television and told the nation that America and the Soviet Union were in the midst of a tense stalemate at sea—what history remembers as the Cuban Missile Crisis.

In a brazen show of bravado, the Soviet Union, with the approval and complicity of Castro, had established a massive military base on the island, just ninety miles from the United States. By the end of the buildup, it held more than sixty thousand soldiers, officials, and technicians. Of much greater concern to the United States, though, was the construction of a nuclear missile base and an electronic listening post for eavesdropping on American military communications.

For thirteen agonizing days in October, the world hung in the balance, teetering on the edge of a nuclear war between its two most potent superpowers as Kennedy and Khrushchev played a dangerous game of brinksmanship. Most certainly, neither wanted to cross the line into atomic conflict, but neither could they find a way to back down. Kennedy called for a strict naval blockade around the island, and the world watched as massive destroyers locked in a dangerous game of dodge-and-parry, with the Soviets determined to punch through and the Americans equally determined to fend them off.

The standoff only served to increase tensions between Kennedy and the military, which advocated an immediate offensive strike against Cuba. They were convinced that a direct showdown with Castro was the better course of action. Kennedy, however, kept his own counsel. He wanted to avoid a war with the Soviets, especially one with the possibility of turning nuclear, with catastrophic consequences for mankind.

Finally, using back-channel communications involving his brother Robert, the attorney general, and the Soviet ambassador, the two world leaders found a way to defuse the situation and still save face. The world could breathe a sigh of relief. So, too, could Castro. He may have seemed merely a pawn in the contest between the two great powers, but he managed to secure a win that would keep him in power for more than fifty years.

Khrushchev agreed to withdraw his nuclear missiles and Il-28 warplanes; Kennedy agreed never to invade Cuba and not to help any anti-Castro exiles who might try. The end result only served to solidify the rancor Cuban exiles had for Kennedy. From what I could tell, it had a similar effect on Bishop.

I grew to have a more favorable opinion of the young president as the years went by. I began to appreciate the intensity of his efforts to ratchet down the dangers of the Cold War, to bring about the first nuclear test ban, and to lead the United States toward the loftier goals that his successor would proclaim as "The Great Society."

At the time, though, I agreed with Bishop that this rich Massachusetts liberal had just handed my homeland to the Communists and left those of us who fought for its freedom in the same position he had the invading exiles at the Bay of Pigs—on our own.

So we continued our attacks. And our announcements. And our leaked information to the various federal agencies keeping track of our activities.

Still, nothing from Kennedy.

Then Bishop had another brainstorm. "Let's lay it on his doorstep next time," he said. "Next time, make sure to hit a Russian ship. Hard. Then, you tell the whole world about it—in Washington, D.C."

It happened in March 1963. As the night of the 17th gave way to the early morning of the 18th, two of our boats—a wood and Fiberglas twenty-five-foot speedboat and a twenty-one-footer—slid into the harbor at Isabela de Sagua, about 180 miles east of Havana. The bigger boat sported a ninety-five horsepower Mercury engine. The smaller one, fitted with twin inboards, could do better than thirty-five knots on a run. Each carried more than a dozen men with BARs and M1 Garand rifles, along with two moveable 20 mm cannons. One group went ashore to attack the heavily fortified Russian Technical Camp on one side of the harbor; the other moved across the port to shell a Soviet merchant ship, the *Lvov*, at anchor nearby.

Somewhere between six and a dozen Russians were wounded; an unknown number were killed. The ship's smokestack and bridge suffered heavy damage.

The following day, I faced reporters from around the world in a press conference at the Roger Smith Hotel, one block from the White House. I deliberately used a government translator. Reporters from the *New York Times*, the *Washington Post*, and several other major U.S. newspapers showed up. So did representatives of the Soviet news agency TASS. I answered their questions with what I hoped was an appropriate dose of insolence.

As Max Frankel of the *New York Times* told it: "Their purpose, they said, was 'to wage psychological warfare against the Government of Premier Fidel Castro and the Soviet troops supporting him.'"

And, I said, the raids would continue.

Bishop believed it would be a direct shot across the bow for the Kennedy administration, and a slap in the face for the Soviets. He was wrong. It was a dud. Prime Minister Khrushchev doubled down on his Cuba strategy and completely ignored us. So did Kennedy, publicly. The administration issued a statement that allowed it to condemn us while avoiding any responsibility.

A State Department response claimed to have no knowledge of the raid, but said that it "reinforces our belief that the irresponsible and ineffective forays served to increase the difficulty of dealing with the unsatisfactory situation which now exists in the Caribbean."

When pressed, the administration insisted there was nothing they could do. The attacks had all been planned and launched from bases outside of U.S. territorial limits; hence, outside its jurisdiction. Therefore, we hadn't violated the Neutrality Act. Or any other U.S. law. So, publicly at least, they maintained that they didn't have any authority to stop us.

Privately, it was another story. The president directed federal authorities, including the Coast Guard, to shut us down. Working through diplomatic channels, they alerted the British that we were running our commando raids out of bases in the Bahamas.

The British Navy seized our ships, confiscated our weapons, and kicked us out of our island hideaways with a stern warning to go back to the United States and never return. In April, the U.S. Coast Guard arrested Eloy Menoyo and four other men after a sea chase involving boats and USCG planes. They brought them back to the immigration detention center in Opa-locka, just north of Miami.

Then the United States imposed its own restrictions on us. All of us were required to register with federal authorities. Our movements were limited. I wasn't allowed to leave the South Florida county where I lived without prior permission, under penalty of arrest.

"Don't worry about it," Bishop said. "It's just for show. So they can say they did *something* to stop you."

He must have been right. We knew there could be no more raids on Cuba, or ships. We switched our emphasis back to Eloy's original plan, to secret a core cadre of counterrevolutionary fighters into Cuba, to launch a guerrilla war. I continued to travel unhindered to meet with exiles from New York to Los Angeles, Chicago to San Juan.

And I traveled to meet Bishop wherever he wanted, whenever he wanted.

So, a few months after Eloy's arrest, when Bishop sent the message that he wanted to see me, I boarded a plane for Dallas without hesitation.

He had summoned me to Dallas before. Several times. So often, in fact, that I came to believe Bishop was from Texas. It was only much later that I learned that David Atlee Phillips—the man I knew as Bishop—was, in fact, raised in Texas. In his memoir about his time with the CIA, Phillips wrote that he was born in Fort Worth and attended Texas Christian University before heading off to World War II . . . and then his espionage exploits in Chile, Havana, Miami, and elsewhere.

Bishop asked me to meet him downtown, in a hotel lobby in one of the tallest buildings I'd ever seen outside of New York City. There was nothing unusual in that. Bishop seemed to prefer conferring in public places, and office buildings and hotel lobbies stood right near the top of his list.

I don't recall if he said the name of the building where he wanted to meet, or just gave me the address. But it's hard to mistake the forty-two-story Southland Center for any other edifice. At the time, it was the tallest building west of the Mississippi, and it absolutely towered over everything else—in fact, it's still the tallest building in Texas. It was known for the observation deck on the top floor, and for its unmistakable façade—curtains of glass walls and, what I noticed most, shimmering blue Italian glass mosaic tiles.

Bishop was already there. The lobby was busy, full of people, but I spotted him standing in a corner, talking to a young, pallid, insubstantial man. He didn't speak when Bishop introduced him to me, or at all for the rest of the time we were together. He seemed shy, and awkward. Like he felt out of place. I noticed his receding manner even more because it was such a contrast to Bishop's natural, self-assured presence. He attracted attention because he was trying so hard not to.

I don't remember if Bishop introduced him by name. He might have said, "Tony, this is Lee. Lee, Tony." But I am absolutely sure that "Lee" said nothing. Not a word. Not even "Hello." We shook hands, but he didn't talk.

We stayed together in the lobby for about five more minutes, "Lee" awkwardly quiet, while Bishop talked to me in vague, general terms about the situation in Cuba. I answered in a similarly conversational manner. I didn't really expect Bishop to say anything more specific in the other man's presence. I guessed he was just trying to not seem rude by having us turn and walk away immediately. But the minutes ticked by uncomfortably as it became painfully clear that "Lee" was not going to take any opportunity to join in the conversation.

Finally, Bishop said something like, "Well, don't let us keep you, Lee. I'm sure you have other things to do. Tony, do you want to get a cup of coffee?"

I said I did, and the three of us headed for an exit.

A teenaged couple was coming in as we got to the glass doors.

The boy, Wynne Johnson, told me recently that he remembers it clearly.

He was fifteen that day in 1963 and had his sights on the girl he was with. He wanted to show her a good time, he said, so he invited her to the Southland Center. They had been there before, but he liked impressing her by taking her up to the observation deck for the best view in Dallas.

He's pretty sure the day was September 7, 1963, eleven weeks before Kennedy's assassination. He arrived at that conclusion because, he said, he knows it had to be on the weekend. He and the girl got there by bus, and there wouldn't have been time to get there after school during the week. He figures it was Saturday and not Sunday, because the buses were running. The library was open. So was the Southland Center. He knows it was at the beginning of September, because school had just started.

That matches my recollection, too. I don't recall the date, or the day of the week, but I do remember it was near the end of the week, and near the end of August or beginning of September.

Wynne said he and the girl came in through the Olive Street door. It led into a long hall and through to the ground floor lobby. It had glass doors at the end, and, as Wynne recalls, when he and the girl entered the lobby, there were three men walking toward them. The one who looked oldest and "in charge," in Wynne's words, spoke to the young couple.

"Excuse me," he said, "can you tell me if there's a coffee shop nearby?"

Wynne remembers that there was a young man next to the one who spoke. When Wynne finally told his story publicly, more than fifty years later, he said the young man matched the description I gave. He was "a pale, slight, and soft-featured young man."

The girl answered. She said she'd seen a coffee shop outside, on her way in. The girl pointed the way to the diner, and the two groups went their separate ways.

Eleven weeks later, the girl thought she saw the youngest of the three men from the Southland Center again. On television. His name, the newscaster said, was Lee Harvey Oswald.

When the girl told her mother this, she asked Wynne to come over as soon as possible. Then she told him and her daughter, in no uncertain terms, not to tell anyone that they had seen a man who looked like Oswald with two other men that day. Never.

"They could kill you," she said.

Wynne did as he was told. He wiped it from his memory, until he read Gaeton Fonzi's *The Last Investigation,* which dealt with the House Select Committee on Assassinations' probe of JFK's murder. As Wynne read the book, the memory of that afternoon came flooding back, triggered by two tiny details Fonzi included—that the meeting had occurred at the Southland Center, and that Bishop and I went to a coffee shop after we said good-bye to the man named Lee.

I vaguely remember Bishop briefly speaking with a girl as we were leaving. I don't remember Wynne Johnson. It doesn't matter. He remembers me. And Bishop. And Oswald.

I remember meeting Oswald, too. Without a doubt. And I remember my shock when I later saw his face on television after Kennedy died and heard he was accused of being the assassin. I recognized him immediately. He was, without question, the same pallid, pasty-faced man I had seen eleven weeks before at the Southland Center, in the company of Bishop.

I knew I wasn't mistaken. Bishop himself taught me how to notice and remember faces.

I also knew not to mention it to anyone. Definitely not to Bishop. The girl's mother was right. I didn't know if Lee Harvey Oswald killed the president. I still don't. But I had no doubt that being an eyewitness who could connect him to someone in the CIA was extremely dangerous.

My foreboding intensified after I returned to Miami.

Just a few days after I got back, a customs agent from Key West came to see me at my home. I knew him. All the anti-Castro activists did. César Diosdado was sort of the unofficial gatekeeper. He patrolled the Keys in his squad car, monitoring the places where we launched our boats, looking for violations of the Neutrality Act. That was a U.S. Customs responsibility. That was his job. He wasn't a bad guy, or mean about it. But people in the paramilitary community suspected that he really worked for the CIA.

If I'd run into him in the Keys, doing his job, it wouldn't have been odd at all. But it was a long way from the Keys to my house. And for him to show up out of nowhere, after Kennedy had been killed, asking if I knew anything about the assassination or Lee Harvey Oswald, was beyond peculiar.

It wasn't, he said, an "official" visit. "They just wanted me to ask around, to see if anybody knew anything, that's all."

"Of course. I understand," I told him. "But, no, I don't know anything about that."

"You ever meet him, Oswald? Or know anybody who has?"

"No," I lied, just like I figured he was lying to me. "Never. Why? Had he been in Miami?"

"Just asking," Diosdado said.

A few weeks later, in early 1964, Bishop came to Miami. He asked me to meet him at our usual spot, Parque de las Palomas, Bayfront Park, downtown. Bishop and I always met there. I didn't mention Diosdado, or our meeting in Dallas, or Oswald. Bishop did.

He had a request, he said. There had been talk about Oswald visiting Mexico before the assassination, that he met with a Cuban couple there. Bishop said he remembered that my cousin, Guillermo Ruiz, worked for Cuban intelligence in Mexico City.

"I understand he likes money. He likes living the good life," Bishop said. "Do you think he'd sign a statement saying that he met with Oswald in Mexico? For money?"

"No," I said. "I don't think he would accept any payment. I think he's really a Communist. He's faithful to the party."

"Well, I'd like you to ask him anyway," Bishop said. "Ask him what it would take for him to tell us about Cuba's involvement in Kennedy's death."

"OK."

"And Tony," he said. "Keep this confidential."

Some time went by before I got the chance to ask Guillermo. Before I did, I went back to Bishop. I asked him if he still wanted me to look into that "confidential matter."

I remember his answer because I'd never seen Bishop react the way he did. He jumped. "Forget about that," he said. "Just act like it never happened. You make believe I never asked you to do that."

We never talked about Oswald again. I focused on Cuba and Alpha 66. Prevented from making more raids by sea, we turned our attention back to Menoyo's original plan to create a guerilla insurrection in Cuba.

We used a totally different approach than we had with the hit-and-run assaults.

"We'll land in the south," said Menoyo. "In Oriente. We'll make our way up into the mountains to establish our base. Then we bring together our people on the island and begin our fight."

He wanted to use small infiltration teams, he said. Separate ones, on separate days. That would make it easier to filter men up to the staging point undetected. If any of them did get caught, it wouldn't jeopardize the entire operation. The trip would be too long if they started from the Bahamas, as we had in the past. There'd be too great a risk of being spotted by Cuban patrol boats on the journey south, then east around the fat tip of the island, and west along the southern coast to the chosen landing place. Plus, they'd have to avoid being seen by the Marines at the U.S. base at Guantanamo, or any of the Navy vessels traveling to and from its port.

"We need to make the run as short as possible, to avoid being seen," Menoyo said. "We need a jumping-off point. As close as possible. In the Dominican Republic."

The idea had other advantages, as well. It would be easy for the men to fly to Puerto Rico on commercial airlines, a few at a time, without arousing suspicion. From there, we arranged with fishermen to take them across the Mona Passage in groups just as small. The turbulent channel between Puerto Rico and the Dominican Republic was a notorious smuggling pass, but in the other direction. Dominicans trying to get to the United States paid exorbitant sums to be transported to the western beaches of Puerto Rico. Fishing boats heading west, toward the Dominican Republic, attracted much less notice.

In addition, once the men got to the Dominican Republic, it would be a relatively simple matter for them to acquire the boats and food and other supplies they would need before venturing to Cuba.

Plus, Dominican government officials were famously pliable. It wouldn't be hard to get them to look the other way, or even help, as we established the Alpha 66 training base and made our preparations. We called the plan "Omega." The beginning now had an end.

The military junta that ruled the Dominican Republic authorized us to set up our base and designated an Air Force colonel as our liaison. We chose Punta Presidente, an uninhabited tongue of land jutting into the sea on the country's north shore. A part of what eventually became a national park, it was isolated, and easily cordoned off from prying eyes. It sat on an inlet that provided a sheltered natural harbor, with ready access to the sea. And it sat almost directly in line with the city of Santiago on Cuba's southern shore.

By the end of 1964, the preparations were complete. Our men had spent months training. We had boats in place and ready to go, well stocked with ample supplies of fuel, food, and ammunition. The first team, Menoyo decided, would slip into Cuba at the end of the year. He insisted on being part of it.

"I can't ask my men to do what I wouldn't," he told me. "I'll lead the way."

He took three men with him. Four weeks after they landed, on January 24, 1965, a Cuban patrol captured them as they rested on a mountain slope. The plan had been discovered almost immediately after they disembarked. They had been dodging ambushes ever since, desperately ducking into the thick brush to evade the helicopters and planes hunting them from above, and the thousands of troops combing through the tropical terrain for them.

With dozens of guns aimed at them, they surrendered. Menoyo spent twenty-two years in prison in Cuba. He was one of the original *plantados*, refusing to perform labor or wear a prison uniform, insisting he was a political prisoner, not a criminal. He was beaten so severely he lost his hearing in one ear and his sight in his left eye. Still he refused.

"I spent twenty-two years in prison," he said when he was finally released. "Twenty of them in my underwear."

Menoyo's capture was a crushing defeat. Our plan for overthrowing Castro and freeing Cuba had been destroyed. I was devastated. I was exhausted. And, after five years of sacrifice and risk, I was disillusioned. I quit Alpha and moved to Puerto Rico.

For Bishop, too, it was clear that the anti-Castro cause was going through its worst moment. Nothing seemed to go right. But rather than just letting me quit, or take an extended break, Bishop suggested I focus on other targets. I was his sleeper agent. At some point, there might be other ways to defeat Fidel Castro, outside of Cuba.

Castro always maintained a special relationship with the leaders of the Puerto Rican independence movement. Puerto Rico enjoyed a special status as a U.S. territory since gaining its independence from Spain with the Americans' help. That brought certain benefits but also kept it in an uncomfortable legal limbo—not fully a state, and not its own country. That status has been the cause of often-violent division between the factions supporting the status quo and those known as "nationalists," seeking to sever the bonds with the United States and establish Puerto Rico as a fully free country. The nationalists have on more than one occasion turned to violence for their cause.

As far back as 1950, a pair of rabid nationalists attempted to assassinate President Harry S. Truman. Armed uprisings broke out the same year in multiple cities across the island, and nationalists intent on assassinating the governor attacked his residence in Old San Juan. It took the Puerto Rican police, National Guard, and U.S. Army troops to quell the revolt. Twenty-eight people died, forty-nine were wounded.

Four years later, another group of nationalists sneaked into the Capitol Building, unfurled a Puerto Rican flag from a gallery overlooking the 240 gathered representatives on the floor of the U.S. Congress, and opened fire with semiautomatic pistols. Five representatives were wounded, one seriously.

Other, much less publicized incidents of violence plagued the island at home, and the issue remained tendentious and volatile in

1965, around the time I gave up my paramilitary efforts and established myself as a sports and concert promoter in San Juan.

It was the end of my time with Alpha 66, but not with Bishop. Concerned about Castro's influence leaking into Puerto Rico through its radical elements, he approached me with a new way of continuing my service to him. He asked me to use my abilities and contacts to infiltrate the Communists in Puerto Rico and to keep tabs on their activities. My work as a promoter for sporting and musical events would serve as the perfect cover, he said.

Bishop was aware that the heads of the Puerto Rican nationalist movement had a pact with Fidel. They received financial support and training from Cuba to help them convert part of the island's youth into expert terrorists. Fidel gained a valuable toehold to extend his global ambitions. It was a long-term project. They proposed creating a climate of solidarity in countries throughout the Third World, using the rallying cry that Puerto Rico was a long-suffering colony held against its will, and that its people ardently desired independence.

Bishop told me not to try infiltrating the Communists myself. I should select a couple of youths to do it for me.

"You direct them and guide them," he instructed. "There's no one else I trust with this responsibility. Remember, Tony, this is a universal struggle. Every time you hurt the Communists here, you're hurting the ones keeping your homeland from being free."

It wasn't hard to find two willing participants. As I built and extended my personal business, I ran them as my own "assets," to use a term people like Bishop and the CIA like to use. They were my covert field operatives, gathering intelligence and reporting back their findings.

Through them, we learned the operations of multiple nationalist organizations, and how the Communist Party used them as fronts to further its own devious ends. In the contorted political environment on the island, the Communist wolf sometimes dressed as a nationalist sheep and sometimes played the part of a beneficent socialist. There was no hint of dictatorship mentioned; they offered delivery.

I found myself living a life much like the one David Phillips said he had in Havana. My work as a promoter allowed me to travel freely, and to keep my own hours. That allowed me to work as a part-time intelligence agent, and to meet as necessary with Bishop during his frequent trips to San Juan.

It also allowed me to make a pleasingly decent income, and provided the luxury of meeting a variety of sports legends including Roberto Clemente, Orlando Cepeda, Johnny Bench, and the then-future Hall of Famer Carl Yastrzemski.

By 1967, I had expanded into operating the concessions at Hiram Bithorn Stadium, an eighteen-thousand-seat open-air facility that served as San Juan's principal venue for everything from major league baseball and wrestling matches to concerts. The beer, food, and soda sales I controlled yielded $10,000 a month.

Near the end of that year, however, it came to an end.

I got an urgent message from Bishop. The Communists had discovered my intelligence activities, he said. He feared they would kidnap me and try to pry secrets out of me. According to his sources, Bishop said, one of my moles had been discovered and might have divulged my name. Cuba had ordered the head of the notoriously violent Los Macheteros to have me watched. They had a reputation for bombings, bank robberies, and murder. Kidnapping would be one of their lesser crimes.

I began carrying a gun and always went around in the company of another person, to make an abduction more difficult. Cuba found another way.

Funny, the way memory works. I remember the day distinctly, a clear and sunny Saturday, under a great blue sky. I don't remember the date.

There was a wrestling match coming up that evening, so I went to the stadium early to make sure everything would be ready for that night. I came through the ticket gate and into the big lobby where the concession stands stood. On one side there were large freezers where we kept our beer and food. We handed it out from there to the independent vendors, who would sell it and bring back our profits.

On the other side lay the way to the locker rooms, where the baseball players and wrestlers changed before and after events.

The locker room was divided into two parts. You came through one door into the first section. Then there was another door, leading to the room where the lockers were. That's where the athletes changed clothes. The wrestling match was still hours away, so the locker room was empty.

I was directing work at the concession stand when a stylishly dressed young woman came up to me.

"Excuse me," she said. "Are you Mr. Veciana?"

"Yes," I answered.

"You're needed in the locker room," she said. "They need to see you."

She was very friendly and very polite, but I didn't recognize her.

"Who?"

"Ramón," she said. "He said it's urgent."

"I'll be right there," I said. Ramón was the code name for one of my "assets," a way for me to know that it was really him sending the message. If he needed me urgently, it had to be important.

I put one of my employees in charge of the concession stand and headed into the locker room. What happened next might have been plain luck, or a miracle.

I stepped through the first door and was just about to push open the second one when a bomb went off inside the main locker area. The blast threw me back and away from the inner door. I landed on my back on the floor, staring at the closed locker room door, too stunned to move. That turned out to be another piece of luck. About fifteen seconds after the first explosion, a second bomb went off. It was clearly timed to finish the job.

If I had been on the other side of the second door, inside the locker room, it probably would have. The second one seemed more powerful than the first. It tore the lockers to shreds and turned chunks into shrapnel that left gaping holes in the walls. The second door leaned off its broken hinges. The heat from the blast started a fire. I continued to lie there, dazed but, astonishingly, uninjured, as smoke rolled out and over me and began to fill the room.

One of my workers found me there. He had come running at the sound of the blast. Now he lifted me up and led me out. I refused to go to the hospital. I just wanted to go home.

Later, a friend told me, "You've got more lives than a street cat."

I laughed, but in my heart I knew that even street cats don't live forever. I had been lucky, but I knew they would try again. So did Bishop.

He came to see me a short time later. He said what we both knew. "You need to leave Puerto Rico."

"Yes," I said. "I guess I'll go back to Miami. I'll be with my family there."

"Or," Bishop said, "you could try someplace new. South America."

"Doing what?"

"I have something in mind I think will be good for both of us."

chapter 8
THE MYTH OF EL CHE

THERE WAS AN opening, Bishop said, in Bolivia. Working for the U.S. government. It meant going back to my banking roots, as an economic consultant for the Bolivians. It paid what was then a prodigiously satisfactory salary—$30,000 a year—in a place where a couple of hundred dollars a month put a family in the upper class.

It seemed perfect. It would take me away from Puerto Rico and reunite me with my family, in a place where we all could live comfortably once again.

It was also a place, I would soon find out, that would lead me to cross paths with Che Guevara once again and give me a second chance to kill Fidel.

When Bishop first suggested it, though, I wasn't so sure.

"Bolivia?"

"Yes, Bolivia," he said. "I think you'd be perfect for the job."

"Bolivia?"

He must have read the look on my face. I'm sure it looked something like shock, disappointment, or bewilderment. Maybe all three.

"Look," he said. "They want to meet you. Go for the interviews, see what you think. I think you might be surprised."

"What about the travel restrictions?" I asked. "I'm still not supposed to leave Dade County."

"That hasn't stopped you before."

"Yes," I said, "but flying around the United States is one thing. This . . ."

"It won't be a problem," Bishop said. "Believe me."

He was right again. I arrived at the U.S. Embassy in La Paz without any trouble, got through the interviews easily, and had a chance to look around the city a little bit, too, before leaving. It was a totally different world for me, and breathtaking—in more ways than one.

La Paz is strikingly picturesque. It rises from a canyon in the wide Altiplano of the Andes, spreading like moss over the surrounding slopes. It is one of South America's oldest cities and, at the time, was Bolivia's largest. It is also one of the continent's most culturally diverse, with three official languages—Aymara, Quechua, and Spanish—reflecting its ancient roots. Descendants of the Incas still travel the city on foot with babies slung in colorful blanket wraps called *aguayos*, draped in their distinctive billowing skirts and bowler hats.

It's also one of the highest cities in the world. A fact especially noticeable to someone like me, who lived his entire life in places where the ocean waves lapped the shore. The thin air at thirteen thousand feet in La Paz left me gasping and dizzy. Everyone told me to rest as much as possible and assured me that I'd get used to it. But they didn't warn me that the change in altitude would affect me in both directions and that I'd feel uncomfortably ill on my return to Miami, as well.

I told Sira, my wife, "Look, compared with here, we'd be going to a country that's fifty years behind."

"You're exaggerating."

"No," I said. "I'm not. There's no television."

That made her pause a moment, I could tell. It was only 1968; television wasn't as ubiquitous as it is today. But between living in Miami and Puerto Rico, it was already somewhat hard to imagine life without it. There was even television in Cuba—from before the kids were born. Tony was now turning thirteen; Ana, twelve; and Victoria, ten.

"That's OK," she said. "We should go. I prefer for you to be at ease, and safe, there than to be here and never come home."

"What about the kids?" I asked. "It's going to be quite a change."

"They'll be fine. We've moved before," she said. "It's a chance for us to be together as a family."

I STILL DIDN'T say yes to the job right away. The salary and the benefits were alluringly attractive; the position, prestigious. I would be working out of an office in the U.S. Embassy itself, representing the American government as an official USAID advisor to Bolivia's Central Bank—effectively, its Federal Reserve.

It would be a triumphant return to my banking roots, in an arguably even higher and more responsible position than I had held working for Julio Lobo in Cuba. I had certainly gone far afield of that in the interim. When I tallied all the guns, bullets, boats, fuel, and food I had purchased for my exile warriors, my current life seemed a barely distant cousin to those earlier accounting days.

And that was what troubled me.

It seemed odd that a federal agency would hire me for such a prominent and important position after such a gap. I hadn't done anything close to certified public accounting, much less economic analysis or banking administration, in seven years. It seemed even odder that my government employers hadn't done a background check. Because, surely, if they had, they would have discovered that I was a known terrorist. I had founded an organization that had launched repeated paramilitary attacks on British, Cuban, and Soviet ships and personnel, and been condemned publicly for it by the United States government.

"I can't imagine they would hire me," I told Bishop.

"Don't worry about it," he said.

HE WAS RIGHT again. I was hired formally in April 1968 and given airplane tickets for the entire family, with all our moving expenses paid.

Funny thing, though—I don't remember ever signing any employment papers. And later, when House Assassinations Committee investigator Gaeton Fonzi looked into my past, he couldn't find any employment papers I had signed either. He found proof I had worked at the U.S. Embassy in La Paz, as I said I had, doing what I said I had been hired to do. But no official employment records signed by me.

LA PAZ WAS extraordinarily cheap to live in, compared to Miami or San Juan. Especially making what would be equivalent to, as this book is being written, almost $210,000 a year.

We lived like royalty. We rented a large five-bedroom house in the posh Plaza Abaroa district, with three servants. One cooked. One cleaned. One helped with the children. Sira paid them $15 a month. And people we got to know there asked her, "Sira, why do you pay your servants so much?"

We traveled often, ate well, and enjoyed life. The kids went to school with the children of wealthy Bolivians and government officials, and it was just a ten-minute cab ride to work. It cost forty cents.

My job, as an advisor to the Central Bank, was to examine the country's banking system, auditing and accounting methods, and other matters related to sound fiscal practices. I was amazed. Television wasn't the only thing missing in the country's development.

I was accustomed to life in Puerto Rico, which is part of the United States. Compared to banking as I knew it, the Bolivian system was so backward, so behind the times. The Bolivians' rules of accounting, looked at through the lens of what were then current standard accepted practices, were archaic.

I made manuals. I created tutorials. I went with my Bolivian associates as they performed audits at banks in cities large and small throughout the country, making suggestions and trying to educate them in modern methods everywhere we went. I got to know the entire country.

Bolivia's general economic policy was no better. When I arrived in Bolivia, a ten-thousand-peso bill was worth, maybe, ten. They finally took the extra zeros off. But when I got there, if you wanted to buy something beyond a pack of gum, you could easily be counting into the millions. People on the street would have to pull out big fat rolls and peel off bills to buy groceries. And all the transactions were done in cash. Only the incredibly large and extremely important businesses didn't do transactions with wads of bills. They would pay in checks. Everybody else paid cash. It didn't matter if they were paying for cigarettes or a sofa. Cash.

Working with the Central Bank put me in a position to develop extensive relationships with tremendously influential members of the business community. In the government, too. High-level people. Working for the American Embassy was very important.

It also allowed me the freedom to do what Bishop had really put me there for. USAID is just a front for the CIA. It put people like me in positions where they had a good reason to be asking a lot of questions, learning a lot about the internal workings of foreign governments and corporations, and developing valuable connections.

So, in my job with the embassy and the Central Bank, I came and went as I pleased. I had no supervisor. I worked, for the four years I was there, without ever having to tell anyone what I was doing. When I had to go to Peru, or Chile, or wherever it might be, I just went. And when Bishop called me at home one day and asked me to meet him in Lima, I got on a plane.

"We've got a Guevara problem," he said.

"But he's dead," I said.

"Only his body," Bishop hissed.

Che had died the previous October, killed in Bolivia while trying to spark a "people's revolution." Instead of that being the end, though, Che was becoming more powerful. The tales of his exploits, his bravado, and his resolve were making him larger than life. He was becoming the stuff of legend. And that, Bishop and I both knew, was dangerous. That would help Communists do with him in death what he had not been able to do in life: win.

By any objective evaluation, Che was a failure. His time as head of Cuba's National Bank and its ministry of industries was a total fiasco. His ineptitude forced his removal. His dream of emancipating the developing nations of Africa ended in ruinous defeat. His vision of liberating the poor countries of South America proved no less calamitous. His effort in Bolivia was moving precipitously toward the same sorry end, when he met his own.

My job was to kill the myth of El Che. Or at least to stop it from growing.

The question was how.

Bishop was an expert in propaganda. He had taught me the power of misinformation. As I had proven with my fake monetary and parental rights "laws," rumors and gossip can be tremendously potent—if people don't know the truth.

Maybe, I thought, El Che could tell them.

WE KNEW THAT Che had arrived in Bolivia almost a year before his death. On November 3, 1966, to be exact, on a flight from Uruguay. He had shaved off his famous beard, along with much of his hair. He dyed what was left gray and slipped through customs using a fictitious name.

He came to spread Cuba's revolution.

It didn't work. Not just because he died. It was failing long before that. It failed because he had overlooked a key factor: this wasn't Cuba.

The same thing had happened in Africa. As he described it in his *Congo Diary*, he had gone there in early 1965 with the same vision. The continent seemed ripe for revolution, in his view, with rampant poverty and an oppressed people held down by colonial rule.

He was right that they opposed their foreign rulers—England, Holland, France, Portugal, and Spain. But he was a foreigner. He didn't speak any of the languages of the people there. He said so himself in his diary.

He had been warned. Egyptian President Gamal Abdel Nasser told him the local populations would think he was trying to be "Tarzan, a white man amongst blacks, leading and protecting them."

He didn't listen. He went. He fought. He failed.

And he fled.

A year later, he turned up in Bolivia, ready to lead another revolution.

He chose Bolivia for reasons that theoretically appeared right. It shares borders with five different countries. That allows a lot of freedom of movement for guerrilla fighters. The country had experienced a socialist revolution, which included nationalizing the mines, but the military had seized control just two years before Che's arrival. It was a country with a large, disastrously poor population, composed primarily of downtrodden indigenous groups. So, theoretically, El Che chose well. Theoretically. But, practically, he was a foreigner.

More than half the population spoke Quechua or Aymara. Che didn't. He surrounded himself with Cubans and complained in his diary that when he went preaching Marxism to the Bolivians, they didn't listen to him.

Once again, he had been warned. Mario Monje, the head of Bolivia's Communist Party, had been to Cuba several times. He praised their revolution. But when El Che came to Bolivia and met secretly with Monje, the Bolivian told him, "Yours is not a revolution for Bolivia."

He didn't listen. Because El Che was a know-it-all. I saw it when I met him in Havana, when he wanted to convince me to give him the names of one thousand accountants to "volunteer" for the revolution. He was arrogant. He was conceited. And he was blinded by it.

He was so sure that everything he said was right that he thought he could do no wrong. I saw it when he was put in charge of the National Bank without being an economist or knowing anything about it. He had such stupid ideas. But nobody could tell him that.

So it was hardly surprising that he didn't listen when he came to Bolivia. He was going to give them a revolution, whether they wanted him to or not.

El Che believed that the victory that he and Fidel had scored in Cuba was a result of the guerrilla fighters' ability. That's true, to a degree. But the victory in Cuba was won under different circumstances from those he faced in Bolivia.

Che Guevara had wanted to be a guerrilla fighter for years before he found the opportunity in Cuba. In the Sierra Maestra, he threw himself into the armed struggle with single-minded purpose and passion.

He was one of the bravest of the fighters in the Cuban Revolution. There is no question about that. He was one of the most disciplined. He was one of the best prepared.

But Cuba was a unique situation. In Cuba, he and his comrades were fighting Batista.

The sorry truth is, Batista was a greedy man. That was his undoing. The rebels fought with their hearts, not just their guns. They gave it everything they had. Batista set a budget for his counterinsurgency battle. Then he siphoned funds from the fight into his own pocket. That was business as usual in Cuba. Batista took a slice of nearly everything, or business didn't get done. His bagmen showed up every night, often still wearing their police uniforms, to carry away his cut from the casinos. Others paid up front.

So much so, it's said, that when Batista fled into exile he took an estimated $300 million with him. Dollars, not pesos.

The war was no different. The war was business. It provided a steady flow of money, much of it from the United States. The Eisenhower administration poured millions of dollars' worth of weapons and support into Batista's coffers. And if the war ended, so did the cash. So when his generals insisted on chasing the rebels into the mountains, Batista said no. Batista didn't pursue the rebels in Cuba because it was against his economic interests to crush the rebellion.

His military vastly outnumbered the rebels and was much better armed. And still the rebels won. Batista put the money in his pocket and handed Fidel Castro the war.

El Che thought that guerrilla guns beat Batista. He didn't account for Batista's greed. And, filled with Marxist passion and flush with victory, he wanted to carry the revolution around the world.

Che was a true believer. He thought Communism would set people free. In truth, Guevara didn't seek power for power's sake. And he openly condemned those he thought did. He even famously criticized the Soviets, calling them just as much imperialists as the Americans. No, El Che was an obsessive extremist about his ideology and thought nothing of killing its foes. But he wasn't a faker like Fidel. Both Guevara and Castro eliminated their enemies. But there was a difference between them.

While Fidel was an opportunist intent on holding onto power indefinitely, Che put an end to his opponents because of his convictions.

No one can deny his spirit of sacrifice, his personal valor, or his dedication to the doctrine of helping the poor. He renounced the benefits of power to live a life of penury and suffering to achieve his goal of ending social injustice. He was convinced that he had a historic destiny to fulfill.

And he was sure that the guerrilla warfare model was the way to do it. But when he took it to Africa, he failed.

He blamed the Africans. In his diary, he called them incompetent, incapable, undisciplined. They were corrupt and unwilling to fight. It wasn't because he was Tarzan. It wasn't because he couldn't even understand their tongues. *They* had lost *his* war.

So, doubled over with dysentery and gasping from asthma, he fled. He spent the next six months recovering in Tanzania and, later, Prague. Then he headed for Bolivia, arriving in disguise in November 1966.

His problems began almost immediately. As Bolivia's Communist Party leader had warned him, the Bolivians he had come to "liberate" proved to be totally unreceptive. As a top-secret internal CIA review of his diary later described it, "the peasant support considered essential to the revolutionary thesis was entirely lacking. It was, in fact, the hostility and suspicion of the Bolivian peasants that forced the band to continue its endless flight through the jungles."

Bolivia may have been full of poor people, but it had a proud sense of self, insular traditions, and a historically understandable wariness of outsiders. While I was there, U.S. Peace Corps volunteers had begun outreach programs aimed at reducing poverty in the country. Poorer families, they noted, typically had six, seven, or eight kids. So the Peace Corps came in and tried to teach the women about contraception. The Catholic Church had a fit. Soon enough, so did the women. It wasn't so much about religion, it was about tradition. And outsiders.

As Che himself would note in his diary, more than five months after arriving, "Not one person has joined up with us . . ."

There was already dissension in the rebel ranks. On March 22, 1967, El Che wrote that he had had a blowout with one of the guerrillas, a man named Marcos, over "a certain lack of respect on the part of Marcos; I exploded and told Marcos and if this were so, he would be expelled from the guerrillas . . ."

A planned ambush that day didn't go off. "The explorers returned at night and I received them with a severe going over," Che wrote.

They were also low on food.

Then, on March 23, they had their first encounter with the Bolivian army, and their first taste of victory. The rebels killed seven soldiers, took eighteen prisoners, and captured a haul of weapons that included mortars, Mausers, and two army radios. "The major and the captain taken prisoners talked like parrots," Guevara crowed.

On April 10, they clashed again with Bolivian forces and won again, although they suffered their first casualties. It was, the CIA would later remark, a "turning point that caused Guevara to view the guerrillas' chances very critically." The original band of fifty fighters was down to twenty-two. Che was so sick that he sometimes couldn't even carry his own knapsack. Food shortages continued.

By the end of August, Guevara wrote of "gray" days and "black" ones, and some when "everything went wrong." Morale and discipline plummeted. Then things got worse.

Che expected the Bolivians to send their elite Rangers after them. He hadn't anticipated fighting the CIA, too. Or, if he had, he underestimated what that would mean. The tide turned before August came to an end.

"After a series of defeats at the hands of the guerrillas, the Bolivian armed forces on August 30 finally scored their first victory—and it seems to have been a big one," a secret White House memo to President Lyndon Johnson proclaimed. "An army unit caught up with the rear-guard of the guerrillas and killed ten and captured one, as against one soldier killed."

On September 26, Che's entry began, "Defeat."

Dwindling food supplies had taken their toll. The rebels began suffering "fainting spells." They were constantly on the run. Che knew they were being corralled, their chances increasingly bleak.

The hunt for Che brought together the Bolivian Army's elite Second Ranger Battalion unit, the CIA, and, it was alleged much later, Klaus Barbie, the infamous Nazi "Butcher of Lyon," known for personally torturing men, women, and children as Hitler's ranking Gestapo chief in the French town. "The Che claim came from several sources," according to Kevin McDonald, who wrote and directed a feature-length examination of Barbie's activities after World War II, including his time in Bolivia.

I don't know if Barbie was involved in Che's capture. I know he was there in Bolivia at the time. I met him, at the German Club in La Paz. A friend introduced us. He said his name was Klaus Altman. After that, we had beers on several occasions. Eventually he told me his real name, and he told me his version of his time in Lyon.

He didn't mention torture, but he did admit to sending several prisoners to their deaths. He said the French Resistance was killing German soldiers in the city. He wanted to stop them. When people were brought in for questioning, he offered them a choice—talk or die. They either gave him information, or were executed. He said there were always plenty of people willing to throw their principles out the window, to save their lives.

That was his version of events. After Nazi hunters found him in Bolivia, he was accused of sending as many as 14,000 people to their deaths, convicted of war crimes, and sentenced to life in prison.

I didn't know any of that when we talked. But he told me a lot about gathering intelligence, and learning enemy secrets. He gave me a bit of advice I never forgot. "The best way to get results," he said, "is to infiltrate the enemy's ranks."

Che Guevara made his last journal entry on October 7, a day spent "without complications, even bucolically . . . until an old woman shepherding her goats came into the canyon and it was necessary to apprehend her."

They questioned her, then turned her loose, and gave her fifty pesos "with the request that she not say a word, but with little hope that she would keep her promises."

Guevara's premonitions came true. The following day, one thousand eight hundred Bolivian special forces members surrounded the rebels in the ravine where they were camped. The guerrillas were down to seventeen men.

Guevara fought anyway, until his gun malfunctioned. Then, one of the soldiers later said, he threw up his arms and shouted, "Do not shoot! I am Che Guevara, and I am worth more to you alive than dead."

The Americans wanted him kept alive, so they could take him to Panama for questioning. It didn't happen.

The Bolivian army held a press conference two days later to announce that El Che had fallen into a coma when captured and died of his battle wounds shortly thereafter. It wasn't true. He was dead, but that's not how it happened.

El Che was bound and taken to a schoolhouse in a nearby village, where his wounds were bandaged and Bolivian officers attempted to question him.

A CIA special activities division operative, a Cuban exile named Félix Rodríguez, had accompanied the Bolivian Army's Second Ranger Battalion on the hunt. He was one of the last people to speak with El Che, on the morning of October 9.

They talked about Cuba, and Castro, and the Congo; about Camilo Cienfuegos and the Bay of Pigs; about the treatment of guerrilla prisoners on the island; and about the future of the guerrilla movement there.

Then the order came from Bolivian Armed Forces Headquarters to execute El Che. Rodríguez was the one to receive it. He knew that the United States had helicopters and airplanes on standby to take Che to Panama for interrogation. However, he said later, he decided "to let history take its course."

According to a memo addressed to key U.S. government officials—including Secretary of State Dean Rusk, Defense Secretary Robert McNamara, CIA Director Richard Helms, and President Lyndon Johnson's special assistant for national security affairs—this is what happened next: "At 1150 hours on 9 October the Second Ranger

Battalion received direct orders from Bolivian Army Headquarters in La Paz to kill Guevara. These orders were carried out at 1315 hours the same day with a burst of fire from an M–2 automatic rifle."

BEFORE HE DIED, Che asked Rodríguez to deliver a message: "Tell my wife to remarry and tell Fidel Castro that the Revolution will again rise in the Americas."

To the trembling young Bolivian sergeant who'd been ordered to kill him, he said, "Shoot, you are only going to kill a man."

The order to kill the legendary revolutionary had come from the highest levels of the Bolivian government. Bolivia's president, top military commander, and minister of the interior held a private vote. All three gave the thumbs down.

But Che was right. They killed the man, and gave birth to a legend.

It started with the photograph.

The day after his execution, the military put El Che's corpse on exhibition for the press to prove that he had, in fact, been killed. Photographer Freddy Alborta's image shows the shirtless, shoeless Che laid on a hospital litter, surrounded by armed soldiers and some journalists. His eyes are frozen open, his features soft. He appears heavy-lidded, as if he's just waking, or drifting off to sleep. He appears, in a word, at peace. A Bolivian officer in full dress military uniform appears to be gently patting El Che's head. Army Colonel Andrés Selich, similarly uniformed, touches a single finger to Guevara's bare chest.

Alborta titled the image "The passion of the Che."

It fits. He looks like Jesus Christ just taken down from the cross.

The soon-to-be iconic photo had such an impact. To see this man, the way he looked. You couldn't help but feel sorry.

The myth of El Che began precisely because of the photograph. I couldn't believe the government had permitted it to be taken and, worse, allowed its publication.

The people already doubted the version of the story the military had put out initially, that El Che had been killed in combat. Once they saw the picture, they were convinced.

Sometime after the photograph was taken, Che's hands were severed for purposes of identification and the body disposed of, buried in a secret location in an unmarked grave, so his final resting place could not become a shrine.

These events had all happened almost a half year before I got to Bolivia. United States security officials put a bold face on the death of Che, but they completely misread what would come. After carefully studying El Che's diary, the CIA concluded, "Guevara, his lessons, and his legend were perhaps simultaneously stifled. Though Castro and other revolutionaries may insist that the struggle endlessly continue in his name they must now be having serious doubts about their prospects."

As the stories of the "Glamorous Guerrilla" continued to grow, however, the agency's perception changed. The situation was fast approaching crisis when I got to La Paz. The problem, I felt, stemmed from the fact that people didn't know the truth.

In truth, El Che's diary was a chronicle of failure. The world just had to see it for themselves. But they had to believe that what they were reading were really Che's own words—uncut and unchanged.

Bishop and I agreed that they only way that would happen was if the diary was published by the Cuban government itself. The problem was getting it to Castro.

We knew that the heads of the Bolivian military were already trying to cash in by the selling the diary to a publisher. I heard they were asking for $1 million. Fortunately for us, the business negotiations were taking time, since a lot of money was at stake. I needed to beat the Bolivian generals to the punch—to somehow get my hands on the original diary, and get it into Castro's hands.

Quite honestly, I had no idea of how to do that. But then fate took care of it for me.

Cuba published the diary.

The impact reverberated across Bolivia, including within the country's government. Everyone wanted to know how Castro got his hands on it.

In the midst of that chaos, the story turned bizarre. First, the minister of the interior vanished. Then, when he turned up—spending a week in a London safe house laying out the story—he took credit for delivering the diary to Fidel.

A confidential National Security Council memorandum to President Johnson later explained what had happened:

[Bolivian] President [Rene] Barrientos is facing the most serious political crisis of his two years in office. It stems from the publication of the "Che" Guevara diary, a copy of which was surreptitiously furnished to Fidel Castro by someone in Bolivia.

Since the diary was kept under lock and key by the Army, the finger pointed there, bringing into question the loyalty and discipline of the Armed Forces. This produced a political chain reaction of protest by opposition groups, a police crackdown, threats of strikes and student disturbances, unrest in the Armed Forces, and finally, replacement of the civilian cabinet with a mediocre military one.

In the midst of all this, Barrientos' Interior Minister Antonio Arguedas took off for Chile where he announced that he had been the one that passed the Guevara diary to Castro. The circumstances of his "fleeing" Bolivia, his public statements, and his desire to come to the United States rather than go to Cuba which has been desperately trying to get him, all cast serious doubt on the bona fides of the Arguedas story. It sounds to me as though he agreed to be the scapegoat for his old friend Barrientos in order to take the heat off the restive Armed Forces.

I spoke to one of Arguedas's close advisers, Julio Gabriel García, to see if he knew what had happened. He told me he was the one who convinced Arguedas to send it to Cuba. Arguedas, who admired Castro, sent along another gift, García said: Che's hands. Apparently, Arguedas admired El Che's bravery. He thought he would honor him—one soldier to another—by sending them to be buried in Cuba.

There may have been another explanation.

Arguedas announced that he had been a CIA operative, furthering the intelligence interests of the United States, while he was minister. He had even, supposedly, encouraged the CIA to lend him some of its Cuban operatives "to put some professionalism" into the ministry's intelligence efforts. Julio Gabriel García was one of them, he said.

It's possible, then, that I wasn't the only one working with the CIA to get El Che's diary to Cuba. Bishop, and others, may have entrusted more than one person with the task to multiply the chances for success.

Whether it had the desired effect is a matter of opinion. Che Guevara remains one of the most enduring, and controversial, revolutionary figures. I'm sure that over the years many have read his diaries and found inspiration. Others, like me, see confirmation of his failure.

He even said so himself, in the preface to the *Congo Diary*. It began: "This is the history of a failure."

The Bolivia diary, I am convinced, is, too.

But for many people, there is romance even in failure, if the fight is for a noble cause. And for generations of young leftists around the world, nothing is more noble than the legend of Che Guevara, the selfless son of privilege who gave his life for the revolution.

With the publication of Che's diaries, Bishop pressed me to focus more on what had been my other primary assignment in Bolivia: get close to the generals. Especially General Alfredo Ovando, the military commander-in-chief.

Bolivia had been under military rule since 1964, when Ovando and President Barrientos had jointly assumed power. At the time, Barrientos was the head of the Air Force. They ruled together for a time, then Ovando stepped aside and let Barrientos hold the title alone.

Now Barrientos was under increasing pressure. It wasn't just the consequences of the capture and killing of Che Guevara. His efforts to increase revenues by raising taxes had turned the poor against him. Trying to reduce costs by slashing miners' pay and cutting the mining workforce further undermined his support.

Meanwhile, the economy continued to stagnate. As I arrived in 1968, Bolivia was expected to have a $10 million deficit by the end of the fiscal year, on top of the $7 million deficit it had already had the year before.

News of U.S. involvement in the capture and killing of Che Guevara further eroded support for Barrientos. And when the president's close friend, Interior Minister Arguedas, suddenly announced that he'd been working for the CIA, the public outrage was explosive. The country seemed ripe for a coup, and I'm sure Bishop figured Ovando would be most likely to lead it.

"Get close to him," he told me.

IT WOULDN'T BE easy. Barrientos was good-looking and pleasant, even charming. But Ovando was like social sandpaper—he rubbed everybody raw.

His wife, on the other hand, was the opposite. She was dynamic, sincere, outgoing, and giving. She was involved in a variety of charities, and although he looked none too happy in the pictures of them that appeared in the paper, she made sure that he was on hand at the fund-raisers and galas, dinners and concerts, and all such similar social occasions. She behaved, in essence, like a first lady, even if her husband didn't occupy the presidency. Yet.

Naturally, I realized that the way to get to General Ovando was through his better half. And the way to her was through charities.

I knew I couldn't take a direct line, of course. But I was lucky enough to make the acquaintance of a young man who was the director of culture in La Paz. He was close to her. I got close to him.

I told him that I had been a promoter before and that I was interested in fostering wider appreciation for Bolivia's cultural heritage, through music. It was true. Bolivia had these singing groups known as *peñas nocturnas*, who were nocturnal strolling minstrels, singing and playing unique traditional instruments I had never seen anywhere else. Not just pan flutes, although there were those, too, but also guitars little bigger than ukuleles, made from tortoise shells. The Americans who worked at the embassy and people who came to visit loved the music. They went to hear the different groups again and again.

I thought that rather than wait for the world to come to Bolivia, it might be a good idea to take their music to the outside world.

"Not only will it bring some positive attention," I told my contact, "it could make a lot of money, which I'd like to see go to charity."

"I think it's a magnificent idea," he said. "How can I help?"

"Well," I said, "as you know, I've only recently arrived. I don't know which charity is best. And I wouldn't want to offend someone by picking the wrong one. I think it would be wonderful if Mrs. Ovando chose."

He agreed. And he agreed to introduce me immediately.

Elsa Ovando loved the idea, too. I surprised myself with my salesmanship. David Phillips, who banged on doors as a cemetery plot salesman as a young man in Texas, would be proud. I got my foot in the door, and then got her to open it wide.

She named a charity right away that she thought would be perfect.

"I can even introduce you to them," she said. "And to others who can help, too."

From then on, I made fairly regular visits. The military sentries guarding the Ovandos' front door got to know me. So did the servant who showed me into the living room to wait while she summoned Elsa. We'd chat for fifteen or twenty minutes and I'd be on my way.

I even enlisted Sira's unwitting help. Honestly, there wasn't a lot for her to do while the kids were at school. I got her to invite Elsa to tea, without telling her why it would be valuable.

Occasionally, I'd bump into Elsa's husband while I was there. Over time, he actually began to greet me. Ovando didn't tell me things directly. And I wasn't necessarily trying to turn him into a mole. I would be in his house, and I would hear people talking. An officer might come to see him about some item of business, and I'd pick up bits and pieces. I had to decipher certain things. Then I'd pass them on.

While I was working on that, two scandals rocked the nation. I learned they both might be connected through an urgent call from Bishop.

The first came the year after I got there. Barrientos died unexpectedly, under questionable circumstances. He was on his way back from a meeting when his helicopter crashed. Many suspected it had been downed by sniper fire, that he had been assassinated by someone in the military. Ovando seemed the most likely one behind it, since he stood to gain the most. But he was out of the country when it happened and made no move to prevent the vice president, Luis Siles, from assuming the vacant presidency.

Siles lasted a mere five months. Then Ovando ousted him in a coup d'état. He became Bolivia's president in September 1969.

Shortly after he did, Bishop told me that Barrientos had been involved in a contorted arms deal designed to make a lot of people, including himself, a lot of money. The short version was that Bolivia would serve as cover for a multimillion-dollar sale of weapons headed to Israel. Bishop wasn't sure if his death had something to do with this lucrative transaction, but he knew Barrientos wasn't working alone. Now that he was gone, the others could divvy up his share.

The urgent call from Bishop came after the country's finance minister, Alberto Larrea, disappeared.

"He knows what happened with the weapons," Bishop said. "I need you to find him, before someone else does."

I'd had time to develop some pretty good sources by then. It didn't help. I asked. And asked. Nobody knew where he was.

Somebody did, though.

I heard it on the radio. Larrea had gone underground. He was hiding out at his sister's house. Somebody sprayed machine gun fire through the window of his bedroom in the early morning. They kept firing until they were sure he was dead.

Ovando was considered the most likely to have ordered the hit, but no one ever proved it. I never did get to have a very close relationship with him. In the end, it didn't matter. A year after he'd staged the coup against his predecessor, Ovando was out, pushed aside by his own military. His successor lasted even less time.

Then Bolivia got a strongman, Colonel Hugo Banzer, who had no qualms about using repression to hold on to power. He did, for six years. The man he named minister of the interior was well known to Bolivians, and to me. We'd all seen him before, at least once. Colonel Andrés Selich was the uniformed officer touching his finger to El Che's bare, lifeless chest in the famous "passion of the Che" photograph.

chapter 9
OPERATION CONDOR

THE DESERT SEEMED to go on forever. It stretched from horizon to horizon in every direction, cut only by the ribbon of road I drove.

Baked. Barren. Vast.

The only humans I had seen for at least two hundred miles were the ones in the car with me—my wife, my kids, and the killer.

Only the killer and I knew about the cache of weapons hidden under the back seat, under where my children now sat. There, buried under some clothes to muffle any attention-attracting clatter, rested a Belgian FN FAL rifle with a telescopic sight, two revolvers, and a pistol.

We had chosen the FAL because of its track record and capability: an effective range of six hundred meters, a powerful 7.62 mm shell, sure and reliable—as long as it wasn't used on automatic. Because of its widespread use by NATO forces, it had become known as "the right hand of freedom."

But it was only a backup. The real plan called for the pistol to be the instrument of Fidel's death. The weapon of choice had to be small enough to fit inside a fully operational television camera, to remain hidden until the assassins were close enough, and to fire one or more shots, point blank, into Fidel's throat and head.

It was, once again, my plan. More than six months in the making, it now sped toward its conclusion. Literally.

It was fall 1971, and I was on my way from Lima to Santiago to oversee another assassination attempt on the man whom I'd been stalking for over a decade. Castro was due to arrive for a state visit in the Chilean capital in November, and my killing team would be waiting for him.

Later, looking back on those long hours spent crossing the bleak emptiness of the Atacama Desert, I realized that my obsession had won. My desire to kill Castro had consumed me. I was willing even to risk my children for that one purpose. I had brought them here in the midst of the world's second-largest desert and set them and all of their innocence atop the weapons, without once worrying what would happen to them if the arsenal were discovered. I never thought once about what would happen if we had an accident out there, hours from the nearest town. About how long we would wait before help arrived. About how long we could last. The Atacama is not particularly hot, but it is the driest desert on earth, a vast expanse stretching under a cloudless sky between the Andes and the Pacific. Scientists say that in the span of one thousand years, a mere four inches of rain have fallen there. In some places, not a single drop has fallen in more than four hundred years.

As I drove through the parched terrain, I could believe it. Everywhere I looked, I saw nothing but sand and dirt the color of rust, under a crisp blue sky.

I didn't care.

The desert was not my destination. It was merely a passageway. This was the path to my future, the way to clear my past—the way to rid the world of Fidel Castro.

I held no one to blame but myself for the failure in Havana. I had prepared so carefully. That was my nature. I am a perfectionist. The apartment had been rented and occupied by my mother-in-law for six months to eliminate suspicion. The weapons moved into place with similar care. The escape plan orchestrated in infinite detail, as well.

But I had failed to account for one factor—the men who would actually be in position to pull the trigger. I still couldn't blame them for faltering. I had no idea what it was like to be in their shoes.

I did know the result: Cuba remained in shackles.

The thought had haunted me during my time in Bolivia. Even as I did the work asked of me. The goal remained the same, to topple Castro, and my regular meetings with Bishop invariably brought new assignments with that end in mind.

Still, I could see Communism and other left-wing ideologies taking hold across the continent. Despite Che's death. Despite the efforts to discredit him with his own diary. Allende had come to power in Chile. Fidel had an ally, and hope.

Salvador Guillermo Allende was a Chilean physician and politician, born into a family of upper-class liberals with a history of political activism. He bore a coincidental connection to Castro from birth: he celebrated his birthday on July 26. It was the date Fidel chose to attack the Moncada Barracks in Cuba, launching his uprising against Fulgencio Batista.

The United States despised them both. But Allende may have been the bigger threat.

Castro seized power through armed revolution. Allende became Latin America's first democratically elected Marxist. That meant he was popular, and the tide against capitalism might be, too.

Castro was, relatively speaking, a kid in politics, and a newcomer to Communism. Allende's political career extended over nearly four decades. He began, like Fidel, as a college student and was arrested several times for protesting against the government. After he got his medical degree in 1932, he co-founded Chile's Socialist Party.

In 1938, Allende headed the Popular Front's presidential campaign. He was named minister of health after his candidate won. In that position, Allende was responsible for multiple social changes, including safety laws for factory workers, higher pensions for widows, maternity care, and free lunch programs for schoolchildren. Later, as a senator, Allende introduced legislation guaranteeing universal health care for the country's citizens, the first program of its kind in the hemisphere.

In all, Allende served four terms as a Socialist Party senator, and as a deputy and cabinet minister. And throughout his political career, he consistently denounced capitalism and imperialism.

Allende's narrow victory in September 1970 was his fourth presidential bid. He won by a plurality of just over a third of the popular vote. Still, even though he had the most votes, the United States poured hundreds of thousands of dollars into a propaganda campaign aimed at convincing the Chilean congress not to award him the victory.

The propaganda plan might have succeeded if another CIA-supported effort hadn't exploded dramatically and tragically.

Two days before the Chilean congress was scheduled to confirm the president, the commander-in-chief of Chile's army, General René Schneider, was shot during a kidnapping attempt headed by one of his generals. Schneider was a firm "constitutionalist," believing that the army existed to defend the country, not to interfere in politics. He staunchly opposed the idea of staging a coup to prevent Allende from taking office. The loyal general's death galvanized public opinion and gave Allende the support of the people and the military.

With Vietnam and the Cold War with the Soviet Union raging, President Richard Nixon and Secretary of State Henry Kissinger vehemently opposed the rise of a second Marxist government in Latin America. Nixon ordered the CIA to "make the [Chilean] economy scream" to prevent Allende's ascension, or to unseat him if he came to power.

The agency's deputy director for plans issued clear instructions to the CIA base in Santiago: "It is firm and continuing policy that Allende be overthrown by a coup. It would be much preferable to have this transpire prior to 24 October, but efforts in this regard will continue vigorously beyond this date. We are to continue to generate maximum pressure toward this end, utilizing every appropriate resource. It is imperative that these actions be implemented clandestinely and securely so that the USG [U.S. Government] and American hand be well hidden."

Once Allende took office, Bishop's focus shifted to Chile. So did the assignments he gave me. More and more, I became a courier, delivering cash to Chilean officials and generals collaborating secretly with the United States. Sometimes it was a two-way exchange: I gave them the thick packet of money I carried into the country, and they gave me documents to take to Bishop.

Sometimes I recognized these clandestine operators. Sometimes I didn't. I was often surprised. And, even though I entered and left Chile through a variety of means and with a variety of false documents and identities, I was frequently reminded of the risks.

Once, Bishop sent me with instructions to deliver an envelope stuffed with cash to a confidential informant in Chile's capital. In return, the informant was to give me a sealed packet with documents from the Cuban Embassy and the Presidential Palace. We were to meet at the entrance to a popular movie theater. My contact would wear a yellow tie, with a matching handkerchief in his jacket pocket.

When I saw him, I offered the passphrase, in Spanish, of course: "Brother, we all have to die."

He responded with the correct countersign, "That we already know." Then, he continued: "Do you have the money with you?"

"I do," I said, "and I'll give it to you as soon as you give me the documents."

"How do I know you have the amount we agreed on?"

"I have no idea how much is in the envelope," I told him. Then I slipped. I used a term only a Cuban would use.

"As you'll see, it's pretty hefty," I said. "I imagine it has more than a few 'kilos.'"

Kilos is Cuban slang for cents. Others would say *centavos*. Using it identified me as Cuban, and that could blow my cover.

The informant gave me a wry smile. "Are you Cuban?" he asked.

"No," I answered, trying to recover. "I'm Venezuelan."

His smile broadened and he gave me a wink. "Chico," he said, "you're as Venezuelan as I am Chilean."

Chico was, in its own way, another countersign. It's another typically Cuban expression.

Later, when I told Bishop what had happened, he said, "You made a mistake. He didn't. Let it be a lesson. And don't let it happen again."

When he saw how his words hit me, he tried to soften their impact. "He really is a Cuban," Bishop said. "A very well-paid one. He works in the Cuban Embassy. We've paid him magnificently, but his information is invaluable."

I waited.

"Thanks to him," Bishop continued, "we've learned the exact location of the militia training camps in Chile. And, more importantly, what their plans and objectives are for the immediate future."

It was indeed a lesson. One that could have easily led to my arrest, or my "disappearance." And one that could easily have led Bishop to question my ability. Or, worse, to consider me a risk whose amateur mistakes could expose, and possibly compromise, his plans.

So when Bishop summoned me to Lima for another meeting, I did as I was asked. I went to receive my latest instructions. What he said, though, I never expected.

We met as we always did, in the lobby of a downtown Lima hotel. The places changed, but we could feel secure—just another pair of men in business suits, lost among the many smoking over their cocktails or coffee. This time, I found him at the Hotel Bolívar, sitting under its exquisite stained-glass dome.

"Fidel is going to Chile," he said, "for an extended stay. There will be plenty of opportunities."

I felt a rush of emotion.

"What?" I stammered. "When?"

"The dates aren't set yet. We have time."

I could barely speak. It would be a chance to redeem myself. I had carried the shame for my failure for so long. I saw it when I looked in the mirror. It welled in me every time I heard Fidel's name.

Bishop might have noticed that I was overwhelmed by the rush of conflicting feelings. He might even have recognized the surge of exhilaration that lifted me and left me speechless. Whether he did or didn't, I'll never know. As I stumbled mentally, gathering my thoughts, he spoke.

"Fidel loves the limelight," he continued. "This is a chance for him to shine. There will be plenty of long-winded speeches, lots of press conferences, and lots and lots of posing for the cameras."

He studied me for a moment before finishing.

"Which means lots and lots of chances," he said, "to get it right."

We met again the next day, at a private residence on the outskirts of the city. Bishop wanted to discuss the mission. He called it "Operation Condor."

We talked for six hours—about the known, the unknown, the obstacles, and the possibilities.

Bishop remained adamant about one thing. He wanted the world to know that the assassins were Cuban exiles. The CIA could not be implicated in any way. Alpha 66, he said, should take responsibility.

"I don't understand your insistence on making sure the assassination bear the mark of *anticastristas*," I told him, "and that there be no sign of the CIA anywhere. People are always going to blame the United States. If a jealous woman kills Fidel one day, people around the world will still believe it was the work of the CIA."

He laughed but remained firm. Exiles must bear the blame, not the CIA.

Beyond that, though, little more existed of the "plan." Still, I returned to La Paz practically floating on air. I had another opportunity. All I needed was the means. Bishop had planted the seed. The details fell to me.

I envisioned speeches. Photo ops. Press conferences. Chances.

But how?

Press conferences involved clusters of people, and strict security checks. Photo ops, as impromptu as they might seem to the uninitiated, tended to be carefully choreographed, quick-moving, and swathed in equally tight security measures. Speeches presented the same opportunities as the attempt at the Presidential Palace in Havana. Maybe.

We discarded the idea of a sniper. We believed Fidel wore a bulletproof vest. If so, success would require a headshot, from a hundred yards away. Maybe more.

Also, the balconies on the Presidential Palace in downtown Santiago, known as La Moneda, were very small. It seemed unlikely Castro would appear on such a cramped stage for one of his multi-hour speeches.

But I knew that Fidel loved press conferences. He'd spend hours talking to reporters. If we could get our people into a press conference, they could kill him. They could get right next to him. They'd be too close to stop, and too close to miss.

Bishop liked it.

Now all I had to do was figure out how to infiltrate two assassins into the press corps covering Castro's visit. And how to get their weapons in with them, undetected.

Bishop and I met again. In Lima. In Miami. We still didn't have the assassination plot figured out, but Bishop was pleased to learn that I had addressed another of his concerns.

Even though he gave me more than enough money for the mission, I still collected donations from groups of Cubans in Venezuela and in Puerto Rico—for the "cause." They did not know what was being planned, or where, but raising funds from them would make it easier to link the assassination to exiles when it did happen.

I continued traveling to Chile, spreading Bishop's cash, buying favors and information, making contact, retrieving packages. The trips gave me valuable opportunities to study the workings of Santiago and, importantly, to gauge the efficiency and effectiveness of state security.

So I knew how capable the Chilean Carabineros were. They were no-nonsense, highly trained, and well equipped, and I knew that for our plan to succeed we had to get through that cordon of armed and astute protectors.

The right men could do it.

With a great sense of expectation, I went looking for them. In Miami. I was certain that's where I would find the men I needed— men of action, men of daring, and Cuban.

It was important to recruit Cubans, and not just to give the CIA its plausible deniability. Exiles had the motive. They, like me, had lost their homeland to Castro. They, like me, wanted it back, and they wanted it free. The only way to do that was to eliminate Castro. Their hearts would be in it. That, I believed, was vital. They would be willing to commit. I wanted dedicated men, not mercenaries.

They were harder to find than I expected.

First I spoke with the people from Alpha 66, because they were men of action. I went see one whom I knew to be a courageous fighter, a man who had fought at the Bay of Pigs and in various Alpha 66 paramilitary attacks against Cuba. He turned me down.

"I don't understand," I told him. "You've been to military actions where you could die."

"Yes," he said, "but those had many chances to escape. Here there is no chance. I'm married. I have children. I have responsibilities. I can't just go and give my life, no matter what it would accomplish."

Another concocted an absurd story, apparently hoping to save face. He said he would do the job, but only with this special rifle that he had. Unfortunately, he said, the rifle was lost in the Bahamas, and until it appeared he couldn't do the job. It was just ridiculous.

I left, wondering if I would ever find the men I needed. I told Andrés Nazario, the head of Alpha 66, "We need to look for two people. I need two or three who are willing to do the job."

Then I went back to Bolivia to wait.

I hadn't been back long when I got a telegram from Nazario. In those days it was like that. A telegram. With a message only I would understand.

During my time as a promoter in Puerto Rico, I had represented the famous singer Raphael. Everyone knew it. The telegram I got contained a single sentence: "Raphael is ready to sing."

That meant that they had the people for the assassination. I flew back to Miami.

"We weren't able to find anybody in Alpha 66," Nazario told me. "But there are two people in El Poder Cubano who are willing to do it."

El Poder Cubano was another exile paramilitary group, headed by a pediatrician, Orlando Bosch. Bosch would later gain international notoriety after he claimed responsibility for bombing a Cuban passenger plane. All seventy-three aboard, including the entire Cuban national fencing team, died. It was a terrible thing. I would not have ordered it—all that carnage. I could not have lived with myself if it had come as a result of one of my plans.

But that bombing was yet to come. For now, the group's most recognizable act was firing a 57 mm recoilless rifle at a Polish freighter at the Port of Miami. It was intended as an attack on a vessel doing business with Cuba. The mission failed. The shell plinked off the ship harmlessly. Bosch and eight members of his group, though, were arrested and convicted of conspiring to bomb foreign ships.

One of the men who took part in the attack was Marcos Rodríguez. Now, as his lawyer appealed his conviction, he stepped forward to take part in my assassination plan.

"We begin in Venezuela," I told him. "Then we go to Chile."

"I'll do it," he said, "if you can get me there. They took my passport. I'm under orders not to leave while my case is on appeal."

"It will be taken care of," I assured him.

The other man was Antonio Domínguez. They called him "El Isleño" ("The Islander"). He also had a reputation of being a man of action. I told him, vaguely, what the plan was. He agreed.

I was relieved, but we had to hurry. The clock was ticking. We had six months to go.

I went to Caracas to look for help. Venezuela's capital was home to many Cuban exiles, including the general manager of one of the country's television networks, Venevisión, Canal 4.

I had met Enrique Cuzcó during my days as a promoter, when I arranged for the Cincinnati Reds and Pittsburgh Pirates to play three exhibition baseball games in Caracas. Cuzcó paid for the games to be televised.

Now, on my way back to Bolivia from Miami, I went to him again.

I told him about the plan to kill Castro.

"I can't give you the details," I said, "but the idea is that the people would pass themselves off as journalists, as a cameraman and a reporter."

He eyed me, waiting.

"I need to get them trained," I continued, "so that they're credible. I need you to recommend someone of confidence who can do it."

Cuzcó gave me the name of another Cuban in the city, a man with decades of experience as a cameraman in Cuba and Venezuela.

I checked him out through another well-connected friend. Then, sure of him—or at least as sure as I could be—I went to see him.

"It's expected that Castro will go to a country," I said, "and he'll give a press conference. I want to train two people. When they are there, they need to appear to be journalists."

I could see he was interested.

"I think if we can get close to Fidel, we can kill him," I continued. "But I don't know anything about how those things work. I need to know. Is it possible?"

He paused. Then he nodded.

"Yes," he said. "I participated in the press conference that Castro gave when he came to Venezuela. You can buy a camera and you can hide a small pistol inside."

I leaned closer.

"Go on," I said.

"Before a press conference," he said, "the cameramen have to hand over their credentials and they have to leave the camera. Then the Cuban security people examine the camera to see if there's anything hidden in it."

"Then they'll find it," I interrupted. "What good is that?"

"With a small pistol, you could hide it in a place inside that they'll never find."

I reeled at the possibility. This was it! It could work.

"I'll show you how," he said.

He didn't fail me.

The trainer told me that when Fidel speaks in a press conference, he generally stands a step above, on a raised platform of some kind. The stage—with Castro in the center, surrounded by Chilean and Cuban officials—would be bathed in the bright lights of the cameras, the flashbulbs, and the reflectors. The press pack, however, would be standing in the dark. Here in the shadows, among the crowd of journalists, the assassin could get the gun out of the camera. He could move closer to Fidel. He could get within ten or even five meters, maybe closer. Then he could fire. And not be seen.

But only if he could pass himself off as a journalist and get into the press conference in the first place.

The man I spoke with agreed.

"I will show them how," he said.

The assassins couldn't pose as just any journalists, though. They had to be Venezuelan. That meant they needed to know Venezuela, and they couldn't make the same mistake I had made in Chile. They couldn't use a Cuban idiom. They needed to sound and speak like Venezuelans. They had to say things like *vale* and *chamo*.

They also had to know things about Venezuela, like the cities, important country leaders, and some of the history. That way, they could be believable as Venezuelans if somebody asked them a question.

That would take training. And time.

First, I needed to get the men from Miami to Caracas.

Luckily for me, Venezuela was a corrupt country. We got each man a blank Venezuelan passport, with a fake name. It was easy. The people from Alpha 66 arranged it. In Caracas, I put the two men in an apartment together and put them to work. They learned to work the camera. They learned to behave as journalists. They learned to "be" Venezuelan.

I went back to Bolivia. Secundino Álvarez, the head of Alpha 66's Caracas branch, sent letters letting me know how things were going.

Three months later, the assassins were ready. I went back to Caracas, to see Cuzcó.

"They're ready," I said. "I need you to give them credentials, identifying them as employees of Venevisión."

"I can't," he said. "I want to help, but if they're caught, or this is discovered—I can't allow the network to be implicated."

My mind raced. Now what?

"But," he said, "here's what I can do: I'll show you what the credentials look like, but you'll have to find a printer and make your own. You take them to a printer, you falsify the signatures, but I don't ever want it to come out that I gave you the credentials."

I arranged to have the fake credentials made, including counterfeit signatures authorizing them. Then I went to see Bishop in Lima. He confirmed that Fidel would be in Chile in September.

"Are you sure that these people will go through with it?" he asked. "You know what happened in Havana."

"I know," I said. "It won't happen again."

He studied me, his unspoken doubts visible in his eyes.

"But," I continued, "I need to give them some kind of a guarantee."

"What?"

"I need to assure them they won't be killed as soon as they do it."

He looked at me for a long time before answering.

"Well," he said, finally, "I'll talk to the Carabineros. I'll have them go and see you in Bolivia, and you can work out the details. They'll call you when they're in La Paz and you meet with them."

Later I would learn that he lied to me. There was no chance that the CIA—or the Chilean security officials involved in the assassination plot—were going to let the shooters live to tell the tale.

Nonetheless, after my meeting with Bishop, two people dressed as civilians came to see me. We met at a cafeteria that catered to the well-to-do, executives, and diplomats, a few blocks from the U.S. Embassy in La Paz. They said they were from Chile.

"They sent us to talk to you," one said. "We are with the government, but we are anti-Communists. Tell us about this assassination attempt on Fidel, where and when it's going to happen."

I smiled.

"Well," I began, "if I tell you . . ."

I shook my head.

"It's not that you guys will betray me," I went on, "but if the word gets out . . ."

"No, no, no," the first one said. "We're here because they sent us. Otherwise, we wouldn't be here."

"Still," I said, "no matter where or when it happens, my men need to know that your men won't kill them."

The one who did the talking looked me in the eye.

"You can tell those men that the chance of them getting out alive is going to be very good," he said. "There's always the possibility that after they've killed Fidel, Fidel's security people will kill them. But that's not logical for them to do. What's logical is that they will want to arrest them."

He anticipated my question.

"There's no way they're going to escape," he continued. "But I think they have a very good chance of not dying."

"Prison?" I asked.

"For a while. We will worry about saving their lives and keeping them in prison until the situation changes in Chile and they are released. But the thing is that they won't die."

He paused, sensing my doubt.

"They won't. Because they will be the most important prisoners in the world."

That's what I told the men. They would be the most important prisoners in the world. They would be famous.

It was time to move them to Santiago, and to wait for Fidel.

Bishop let me know Fidel's trip had been postponed to November. We put the men in place a month and a half before that. We rented the apartment they would work from even earlier.

Another Cuban I knew in La Paz, Miguel Nápoles, was married to a Bolivian woman. They both helped me.

"You know that your friend is crazy," I told him. "We're going to try to kill him."

"Damn!" he said. "How?"

"That's not important. But I need your help," I said. "I need the three of us—you, your wife, and me—to go and rent an apartment so that when your friend arrives, we'll already have it. If they go to rent it after he gets there, it's going to draw a lot of attention."

The three of us flew to Santiago together. We were there about a week trying to find the apartment. It needed to be in the center of town, not too luxurious and not too miserable. We finally found a place not too far from the Presidential Palace, on Calle Huérfanos, Orphan Street. Since Nápoles's wife was Bolivian, not Cuban, I sent her to rent it.

"Tell the owner that you have some nephews who are coming to live there and that's why you're paying the rent for them."

Then we went back to La Paz, with the key.

With that taken care of, I went to see Bishop in Lima.

I told him I needed a small pistol, two revolvers, and a rifle with a telescopic sight. The pistol was for the camera. The revolvers were backups, in case the men needed them to escape. They could stash them in the apartment, or a car, and use them if they needed to.

The sniper rifle was a different kind of backup. In addition to the apartment, I wanted one of the men to rent a room at the Hilton, across from the Presidential Palace. On the off chance that they heard that Fidel would be speaking there, or even if he launched unexpectedly into one of his marathon speeches on one of La Moneda's balconies, they could go to the hotel, sight the rifle, and, if the conditions were right, take their shot.

Otherwise, they should go with their primary plan.

Bishop told me there were two ways to get the weapons to me. He asked if he could mail them to me at the embassy. He could send them to me in a package mixed with clothes.

I told him no.

"It's too risky," I said. "If they open it for any reason, then what?"

"Well, then," he said, "I can give them to you here in Lima."

"What then?" I asked. "What do I do from there? I don't have anybody in Lima to give them to."

"That's your problem," he said. "I'll let you know so that you can come and pick them up."

I accepted. I had no choice.

Meanwhile, unknown to Bishop, I had gone even further to deflect blame for the assassination from the CIA. He wanted the assassination linked to Cubans. Fine. I wanted it to go beyond that. I would implicate the Soviets.

One of my friends in Caracas learned that a professor who was there from the Soviet Union had actually been a spy in other countries. I sent Domínguez, on a pretext, to meet with him at his home. While they spoke in the garden outside, I had a photographer with a telephoto lens capture their seemingly friendly meeting.

Then I arranged for a fake dossier documenting some of the professor's activities in Venezuela and other places. In it, as well, I included papers giving the instructions for Castro's assassination, apparently on Kremlin orders.

If the assassins died, I'd see to it that the documents were leaked. That way, I presumed, the Soviets would be permanently stained. They'd be suspected of killing one of their allies. I'd sow mistrust, and, with Castro's killers dead, there'd be no one to disprove the Kremlin's role in his murder. The mistrust, I figured, would lead to a breakdown in relations. Without the economic and political support of the Soviets, Cuba would be weakened, and lose its great defensive shield against the United States. Combined with the death of the regime's charismatic head, Fidel, a break with the Soviets would almost certainly ensure the collapse of Cuba's Communist government.

With just over a month left before Castro's visit, I moved the men into place.

I sent Domínguez ahead with his TV camera and his fake credentials. He had no weapons. That way he would get there clean.

I gave him the key, the address, and instructions. "When you get to Chile, you take a taxi," I told him. "You wait there until Marcos Rodríguez gets there."

Then I went to see an engineer I knew in Lima. I felt I could trust him. But I'll tell you something, in this kind of thing, it's risky. You have to take your chances.

"I need you to do me a favor," I said. "Someone is going to come to see you from Caracas. His name is Marcos Rodríguez. I need you to receive him and attend to him because he knows nothing about Lima."

He didn't object. I continued.

"I need you to facilitate the way for him to go by highway from there to Arequipa, in Peru."

"OK."

"Also," I said, "you will receive a package that has weapons in it."

He nodded.

"When you get the weapons, you take care of them. You hide them in a suitcase. You tell me how much it costs for the suitcase, a very well made one, disguised with clothes in it. I'll pay you."

Again, he said nothing. I went on.

"And you give it to him and you set it up so he can make it to Arequipa. With the suitcase."

He met Marcos Rodríguez at the airport in Lima. I believe he even took Rodríguez to stay at his home for one or two days, until he got in touch with me by telephone in Bolivia. Then Rodríguez took the weapons, in the suitcase, and went by bus to Arequipa.

I met him there, with my family, all loaded into my American government-issued light blue 1968 Chevy Impala, U.S. Embassy license plate number 137. When my children and wife weren't looking, I slipped the suitcase under the back seat. Out of sight, but definitely not out of mind.

Then we headed south on the winding road out of Peru's famous "white city," away from its perfectly square city blocks and the unique lava-stone buildings that earned it its nickname, and away from the soaring volcanoes dominating its skyline. We were on the way to meet my destiny, in Santiago. Our route took on us on a meandering, and spectacular, drive from the rugged, lava-covered western edge of the Andes, and down into the jagged strip between the coast and sea that was the Atacama.

Later on, when I took the time to think about it, I thought about how irresponsible I had been. At the time, all I thought was "I have to do this."

It's like a horse with blinders on, only able to look straight ahead to where it has to go. You never stop to analyze the consequences. The person who stops to analyze the consequences never does anything.

So I followed the two-lane strip south from Aqueripa, in Peru, across the border to Arica, in Chile. Neither the killer nor I blinked when the border guard checked our IDs. I shook my head innocently when he asked if I had anything to declare. I offered only a simple smile as he waved us through.

I left my wife and children in Arica—a vacation, we told the kids.

"Daddy has to drive this man a little farther. You stay here with your mother until he gets back. Then we'll all go to the beach."

Miguel Nápoles flew to Arica and met us there. Then Miguel, Marcos, and I drove the narrow highway from there to Santiago, all through the night, the road blanketed in fog.

It took a long time. I ate dinner and breakfast still on the road. Then we drove on, all through the next day, mile after mile after mile after mile after mile, without ever seeing another car.

We got to Santiago at about 9 p.m., hungry. We ate, then went to the apartment on Calle Huérfanos at about 10:00. We parked on the street, with the weapons still in the suitcase under the seat.

"Let's keep an eye on the street," I told Miguel and Marcos. "When nobody's coming, we'll take the weapons up."

Domínguez was already there, waiting. He had the camera. We put the suitcase in the closet, talked a little bit, then slept. In the morning, I took Domínguez and Rodríguez aside.

"You have to get established here," I told them. "You have to go to the presidential secretariat and get credentials."

They nodded.

"Then you have to use them," I said. "You have to interview people here. You have to go talk to government officials. Tell them that you are here from Venevisión. Ask about the economic situation. Ask about agriculture. Ask about the changes they've made since Allende took office last year."

I could tell this seemed like too much bother for them, so I pressed on. I wanted to be clear.

"We have a month before Fidel arrives," I said. "You have to establish yourselves as journalists. You have to use those credentials, and you have to get to know the entire city."

I gave them my phone number, with instructions to give me regular reports.

Then Miguel Nápoles and I left for the long drive back.

CASTRO ARRIVED IN Santiago on November 9, 1971, a revolutionary rock star, making his first visit to South America in more than a decade. It was a chance for him to bask in the adulation of the country's leftists, and for Allende to show that his nonviolent "road to socialism" approach had Fidel's seal of approval.

Fidel landed, however, hoarse with a cold. I got my first frustrated call from his would-be assassins.

"There was no press conference," Domínguez complained.

"There will be," I said. "Be patient. And be ready."

Castro, however, seemed intent on appearing at public rallies, which allowed him to play for an adoring audience but kept the covering press at a distance.

Castro was scheduled for a ten-day visit, and as the first week ticked by, I began to worry that he would leave without giving my team its chance. But Bishop's information that the sojourn would last weeks proved correct as Castro announced extension after extension.

Press conferences, however, remained elusive. Fidel headed off to the country's mining and agricultural regions, donning a miner's helmet for a descent into a coal mine, and a fedora at a farm. He played basketball with nitrate miners in one city and chatted until 3:00 a.m. with army officers in another.

As much as he longed to be the exclusive center of attention, however, Fidel found himself competing with protests and strikes in the politically divided country. Marxist and anti-Marxist youth groups clashed in the streets. Police fired tear gas to disperse a crowd of five thousand women protesting food shortages. The Carabineros arrested more than one hundred rock-throwing rioters in a single night, and Allende declared a state of emergency as the street fights intensified.

I began getting information in advance about Fidel's itinerary as he bounced from factory visit to factory visit, Marxist meeting to Marxist meeting, and rally to rally. Finally, as his stay stretched into its third week, I learned that there would be a press conference in an enclosed place before he departed. The date: less than a week away.

The delay, I felt, was to our advantage. By then, I reasoned, the assassins would have gained the confidence of the security teams, who would consider them true journalists.

I would never find out.

Barely a week before Fidel's scheduled press conference, Marcos Rodríguez called. He told me that Domínguez was abandoning the mission. He was going to Lima. I called a longtime associate, Antonio Arocha, immediately.

"I need you as quickly as possible in Lima," I told him. "I'll meet you there."

Arocha was at the airport when I got there. We waited for Domínguez's plane. We wanted to surprise him. We did. We caught him as he came off the plane.

"Domínguez," I asked, "why did you leave? What happened?"

He clearly hadn't expected to see me there. His answer proved it.

"I had to," he said. "Some of Fidel's security detail knows me. Several of them. If they saw me, they would grab us. It would ruin everything."

I glanced at Arocha. I could read the doubt on his face.

"I didn't want the mission to fail because of me," Domínguez continued. "So I left. But it's okay, because Marcos has already found a Chilean man who is anti-Communist to help him."

"But you two were supposed to do it. It was all planned. You trained for it. How could he go and find somebody else on such short notice?"

"It's all arranged," Domínguez insisted nervously. "He already took care of it."

He looked at Arocha for support, found none, and jabbered on defensively.

"What do you want, for the whole thing to be ruined? At least now we still have a chance."

I was in shock. I didn't know what to say. Arocha and I walked away.

"You can tell he just made that all up," Arocha said. "There's no Chilean. The whole thing is collapsing."

I knew he was right. And I felt myself collapsing, too. After so much planning, after so much preparation, it had come down to the men I had chosen, again. And again, they were failing me. I was powerless to prevent it. There was nothing I could do but wait.

Three days later, I got a call from a doctor in Santiago.

"There's a man here who wants to have his appendix removed," he told me. "Marcos Rodríguez. He told me to call you and tell you."

"He has appendicitis?" I asked.

"Well, yes," the doctor began. "But it's chronic, not acute. He doesn't need to be operated on right now. But he wants us to."

I was devastated. I knew it was an excuse. Rodríguez had concocted an elaborate lie so he could abandon the assassination plot and still save face. They had lost their nerve. I had lost my chance.

"The cost is very low," the doctor continued. "It's $300. But he wants to be operated on. I want to know what to do."

"I'll pay," I heard myself saying. What did it matter? Domínguez was gone. Rodríguez was alone. What would I do if I were in his shoes?

Fidel's luck had held out again. After nearly a month in Santiago, he would be returning to Havana in a matter of days. He had met Peru's president on his way to Santiago. Now, I read in the newspaper, he planned a stopover in Ecuador on his way back. He would spend three or four hours there.

I was desperate. I raced to Miami to see Andrés Nazario. I tried to put together a last-ditch effort to kill Fidel in Ecuador, before he returned to the well-guarded safety of Cuba.

I couldn't. It was too late. The security around the airport in Quito would be too tight. There wasn't enough time to get inside with both weapons and men.

Fidel flew to Havana. I flew to Lima to see Bishop. I had no choice. When I told him what happened, he flew into a rage.

"Cubans have no balls!" he yelled. "They aren't real men. They're cowards!"

He went on, lashing me with his words. When he stopped, his face was hard.

"Kill them," he said. "Make examples of them."

"What?"

"How much does it cost to have someone killed in Bolivia? Two hundred dollars? Pay it. Invite them there and do it."

"But I . . ."

"We can't afford for them to stay alive," Bishop continued. "They're a risk. They can expose the State Department's involvement. They can connect you to the assassination plot. You, an employee of the U.S. Embassy in Bolivia. Think of the damage that will do."

I was stunned.

"But," I said, "we ran the same risk if they had succeeded and survived. They could have talked after they were arrested."

Bishop chuckled.

"Arrested? Survived?" He shook his head. "They weren't going to survive. Their deaths were already arranged. I just never told you."

I don't know if my answer surprised Bishop. It shouldn't have. Even before I had begun my training in Havana, he had looked at the results of my lie detector tests and seen the potential for this. Principles, he had said then, can be a good and bad thing.

"No," I said. "I won't. I can't. I can't order someone's death when I wasn't even there. I wasn't running the risk he was. I don't have the arrogance to order a man's death when I stood at a safe distance, nowhere near the danger he faced."

Bishop looked at me for a long moment. Then he told me to go back to Bolivia.

I didn't know it then, but that was the end for Bishop and me.

chapter 10
IS THAT YOU, MR. BISHOP?

PERHAPS NOT SO surprisingly, my contract with USAID ended just a few months after my tense showdown with Maurice Bishop.

At the end of June 1972, we packed our bags and moved the family back to Miami. I went back to doing what I had done in Puerto Rico, working as a promoter. I divided my time between Miami and Caracas, and dedicated myself to rebuilding a business booking sporting events and concerts.

I also dedicated myself to Cuba. Castro might have gotten away from me in Chile, but my crusade wasn't over.

My contact with Bishop had grown virtually nonexistent since I had left Bolivia. Without him to direct me or to make demands on my time, I went rogue. Maybe what hurt Bishop most was that it took him more than a year to find out.

I went back to old goals, with new methods. I set about creating teams of exile fighters in cells across the hemisphere. My work as a promoter served as a cover and gave me the freedom to travel to different locations where I could meet with contacts and make plans. Just as I had done in Cuba, I kept the cells to a handful of members or fewer, each separate and unaware that other cells even existed.

Bishop's lessons—the conspirator's commandments—served as my guide. Now, though, I added in elements from the experience I had gained since leaving Cuba. Instead of focusing entirely on a single operation at a time, I set simultaneous plans in motion, with overlapping schedules and, sometimes, even overlapping teams.

Some of the missions aimed to pick up where we had left off in Chile. I scanned news reports and tapped into sources on and off the island, trying to learn of Fidel's travel plans as far as possible in advance. I knew I couldn't get to him in Havana, but with some luck and careful preparation, I could be ready for him to come to me. Every state visit, every gathering of leaders became a possibility.

Other missions were intentionally designed with a dual purpose, to inflict damage and to incite outrage. They were what Alpha 66 had done so many times before, aimed at provoking the United States and the Soviet Union into breaking the accord that had brought an end to the October 1962 missile crisis and left Cuba in chains ever since. Kennedy's promise not to invade Cuba remained in effect nearly a decade after his death. But not for me. The superpowers had called a truce; I remained at war.

Within months, the operations were up and running. There were five in all.

THE FIRST ONE involved an assassination, but not of Castro.

Ramiro Valdés was one of the key figures in Castro's government and one of the most hated among exiles. He had been with Fidel since the earliest days of the revolution, joining him in the July 26 attack on the Moncada Barracks. He'd been captured and imprisoned, and as soon as he was released, he joined the fight again. He teamed up with Fidel in Mexico, joined him aboard the legendary leaky ship *Granma* for their invasion of Cuba, and fought alongside him in the Sierra Maestra.

After the revolution's triumph, Valdés took on a darker role. He joined in the tribunals that sent hundreds to their deaths, presiding at summary trials and the firing squads that followed. Then, Fidel placed him in charge of his intelligence apparatus. In many countries, that might mean gathering information to defend the people from foreign attackers. In Cuba, it meant turning its tools of repression and fear against the people, so the government could tighten its grip. Castro made him his head of G2, and later, chief of its even more powerful and insidious counterpart, the Ministry of Interior. Flush with power and an iron fist, Valdés choreographed witch hunts, purges, and disappearances. And, while the full tally might never be known, he was responsible for sending hundreds to their deaths and thousands more to prison.

Valdés had never shown mercy for his adversaries, so now there would be none for him.

Now, in the summer of 1973, Valdés had taken up residence in Paris for an extended stay. A group of anti-Castro activists was already plotting to kill him. That's where I came in.

Carrying it out fell to Juan Felipe de la Cruz and another whom I can't name. The plan called for placing a bomb at the Cuban Embassy, timed to explode when Valdés was sure to be near. It seemed simple enough, but pulling it off would take nerves of steel, steady hands, and unwavering will.

Juan Felipe de la Cruz was the perfect man for the job. He was athletic, educated, and single-mindedly determined to defeat Castro. Born in 1944, the great-grandson of a celebrated colonel in Cuba's war for independence, he was one of the Pedro Pan kids, sent alone into exile by his parents after Castro came to power. He vowed to return to a free Cuba.

In 1970, de la Cruz joined the Cuban Revolutionary Directorate, known by its Spanish acronym, the DRC. He wrote for the exile magazine *Réplica*, took to the airwaves on Radio Mundo, and prepared himself for combat. At the start of 1973, he wrote out his ideology for all the world to see. "There is only one enemy," he declared. "He who impedes a change in the current situation, and in so doing denies the people their inalienable right to the pursuit of happiness by way of their own free will."

De la Cruz never mentioned Castro by name in the credo. He wrote about Cuba. But he made it clear that he was willing to go to any lengths in the "service of the sacred fight for Cuba's freedom. . . . This is our [only] alternative. War without quarter against the true enemies of the nation, in the country and in the city, in the homeland and beyond. By any means and in every form."

So it was no surprise that when the idea arose to eliminate Valdés, by planting a bomb at the Cuban Embassy in Paris, it was de la Cruz who volunteered.

As we put the plan in motion, assembled the materials, reviewed maps and embassy schedules, and went through the myriad other preparations necessary for success, I got a call from Bishop. I was in Caracas. He was, too. He wanted to see me, right away.

He asked me to meet him at the restaurant at the Rinconada race-track. It was an ideal location. Neither of us was known there, and the rest of the patrons were more concerned with their bets and watching the races than they were with what two men having lunch at another table were up to.

I could tell immediately how annoyed he was, and how hard he was trying not to show it. He was dressed well, as always, in sports clothes. He wore dark sunglasses. He didn't take them off. I suspected he was trying to hide his eyes as he studied my reaction to his words.

"You really got me in hot water," he said. "What made you think you could get away with trying to pin the blame for the assassination on the Soviets?"

He caught me off guard. It wasn't a question I was expecting. More than eighteen months had gone by since the failed assassination attempt in Chile. I thought of it as something, if not forgotten, certainly in the past.

"Who told you such a stupid thing?" I asked.

"Stupid was trying to do it," he said. "You know I'm not joking. And, believe me, if you think I'm upset, you should see the people I work for. They're seething."

From what I could see, he was, too. Bishop could barely contain his anger.

"I know everything," he said. "I know you got someone in DISIP [the Venezuelan intelligence agency] to doctor the police records to lay the blame on the Soviets."

"Maurice," I said. "Seriously, I don't understand what you're suggesting."

"Tony, you can drop the act. You know full well what I'm talking about. Do you know the damage you could've done?"

He looked like he was trying hard not to pound the table.

"I can't trust you anymore," he continued. "You went off on your own. Let me tell you something. The private doesn't set the strategy. He follows orders."

He shook his head.

"It's my own fault," he continued. "My people have suspected you for a while. They warned me about you. And I stupidly defended you. You betrayed me."

He could barely contain his anger. I could understand it. If things had gone my way, it would look like he did not have proper control over his asset, like the student had betrayed his master. And if, somehow, the CIA ended up implicated in trying to pin the blame on the Soviet Union, he could be held responsible for a major diplomatic crisis.

"You don't understand," I said. "I wasn't trying to be disloyal. I wasn't trying to go against your wishes."

"Then why did you?"

"Because of Cuba," I said. "You do what you do for money. I do it for Cuba."

"What does that mean?"

"Ever since the Bay of Pigs, we've been on our own," I said. "I've been on my own."

"That's not true," he said. "What do you think Chile was about? We want him gone as bad as you do."

"No," I said. "Not we. You, maybe. Me, yes. But not the United States. They don't care. I do. And if they won't do something about it, I will."

"That's what this is all about?"

"Yes. That's what this is all about."

I couldn't see his eyes behind the sunglasses, but I could see his jaw tense.

"You signed a contract," he said. "You signed a loyalty oath. Do you know what that means?"

"I wasn't being disloyal," I said.

"What do you call it?"

I tried to find words for the answer. They didn't come. It didn't matter. Bishop was done listening.

"Go home, Tony," he said. "Go home."

"What about you?" I asked. "What happens now?"

"Don't worry about it."

I WAS BACK in Caracas again the following month on business. I hadn't heard from Bishop since that day at the racetrack. I had been busy. Fidel was planning a stopover in Georgetown, Guyana, on his way to the meeting of nonaligned states in Algiers. I was going over the details of his scheduled visit, looking for another opportunity to make it his last. I was moving forward on the Paris plan against Ramiro Valdés. And I was also trying to do something for my family. I had set aside time to relax at home in Miami during the month of July. My parents were coming back from visiting Spain. Other relatives, too, were wrapping up vacations in other places. We scheduled a family get-together once everybody got back.

So, on July 7, 1973, I left Caracas on a Viasa airline flight and headed home to Miami. We made a brief layover in Maracaibo before finally touching down at Miami International Airport at 2:00 p.m. I was thinking about vacation. Somewhere else, other people were thinking about me.

I spent the next two weeks trying my best to focus solely on my family and getting a tan relaxing on the beach in Miami. There were occasional brief interruptions as I dealt with some detail or other connected to de la Cruz's imminent trip to Paris, but, for the most part, I was able to enjoy what I thought was some well-deserved time off. The final days of my vacation coincided with the international CPA convention. It was being held that year at the Everglades Hotel in downtown Miami from the 19th to the 22nd of July.

The day before it ended, Juan Felipe de la Cruz boarded a plane to Paris. Three days later, I was under arrest.

It was the last day of our Miami Beach vacation. I loaded the family in the car and headed for home. The police were waiting when we got there. I thought it had something to do with the Paris plot or any one of the other plans in the works, so I was surprised when the police said they were with the narcotics squad.

"Mr. Veciana," one of them said, "you're under arrest for the illegal transportation of narcotics."

"What?"

My mind was racing. It all seemed surreal. Of all the things they might have said that I was under arrest for, drug smuggling was the last I would have expected.

"That's impossible," I said. "It's a mistake."

"You have the right to remain silent. If you choose to waive your right, anything you say . . ."

They asked if it was okay if they looked around inside the house.

"Go ahead," I said. "I have nothing to hide."

They found weapons, and the credentials and passports that had been used in the attempt on Fidel in Chile.

Then they led me away.

I spent two days in jail while my wife arranged bail. I found a lawyer in the phone book.

In what may have been some kind of transcendental irony, I was released on July 26, twenty years to the day from when Fidel Castro launched his fateful attack on the Moncada Barracks. I got a call from Bishop that very same day. At my home. The phone rang at 6:00 p.m. I remember, because he had never called me at home before. Again, he wanted to see me. And again, right away.

He told me to meet him at the Flagler Dog Track at eight o'clock on the dot. The track was close to my house at the time, and clearly the races were in session. The parking lot was crowded. Bishop was sitting in a car waiting when I got there. He got out, carrying a briefcase. Two young men wearing suits stood nearby, just out of earshot.

"Mind if I pat you down?" Bishop asked.

"For what?"

"You watch TV, don't you? I want to see if you're carrying a gun," he said. "Or a tape recorder."

When he was satisfied I had neither, he spoke again.

"What's happened to you, Tony? Drug smuggling?"

"I didn't do it," I protested. "You know me."

"I used to," he said. "At least I thought I did."

"I've been set up," I said. And then an uncomfortable question popped into my mind. "You wouldn't know anything about that, would you?"

"Tony, you've made some pretty serious mistakes lately. I think it would be wise not to make another one. The penalties in narcotics cases can be very severe."

"I'm innocent," I said. "And I'm pretty sure you know that. I think you might have something to do with this."

His brow furrowed.

"You're irrational. What's worse for you is that no one would ever believe that," he said. "There's nothing I can do for you, Tony. Everything is over between us."

I said nothing.

"I trust you won't reveal anything you swore to keep secret, under any circumstances," he said. "There is never a reason that would justify breaking your vow. That's a piece of advice."

"That's advice?" I asked. "Or a threat?"

"Take it any way you like," he said.

He held out the briefcase.

"This is for you. I'm paying you for your work, to the last penny."

"I never asked for money to fight for Cuba," I said.

"Take it," he said. "You'll need it. You've got enough to worry about right now, without having to worry about money."

He didn't shake my hand. He just said good-bye and walked away. The men followed him back to his car. I watched the taillights fade as they drove away.

I opened the briefcase after I got home. It was filled with tight bundles of $100 bills held together with rubber bands. There was a note on top. It read: "Antonio Veciana. Honorarium. $253,000."

I was alone. The kids were asleep. Sira was in the other room. I took the wooden statues we had brought back from Bolivia off the shelf. Hardly anybody realized they were hollow. I packed the bills inside. They'd be waiting for me when I came back for them, I figured. Whenever that might be.

I WENT TO see my attorney a couple of days later to discuss my case.

"I'm innocent," I told him.

"That's good," he said with a smile. "I'm glad. But it doesn't really matter. What matters is if we can convince a jury that you are."

His smile disappeared.

"I'll be honest with you," he continued. "You're facing twenty years in a federal penitentiary. It doesn't look good."

He flipped through some papers in front of him.

"How well do you know Augustin Barres?" he asked.

"Not well, really," I said. "A business associate introduced us. In Puerto Rico. He was involved in some baseball games we handled. Why?"

"He's the one they busted. Selling coke to undercover agents. Seven kilos," he said. "Stupid."

"Yes," I said. "That's what I said when they told me what the charges were while I was in jail."

"He says you're the one who brought the coke into the country. From Bolivia."

"That's ridiculous! That's a lie," I said. "I told them that at the jail."

"He says there were other shipments. A total of twenty-five kilos."

I opened my mouth. He stopped me.

"I know," he said. "It's a lie. You told them that at the jail."

He smiled. I did, too.

Still, he said, it didn't look good. Barres was cooperating with the government. He had given a full statement. So had the third person they charged, Ariel Pomares. He was accused of setting up the sales in the United States, once the cocaine arrived.

My attorney said we'd have time before the trial to examine the government's evidence, and to prepare our defense. Then he stood and held out his hand. We shook.

"There's really not a lot to do until we know more, Mr. Veciana," he said. "Go home. Try to relax."

I couldn't. Even if I weren't facing trial and the possibility of two decades behind bars, I couldn't. Juan Felipe de la Cruz had arrived in Paris.

Up to that point, everything had gone according to plan. De la Cruz had flown to Madrid, then made his way to Paris. He checked into a small hotel on the outskirts of the city, the Oasis, and carefully went about gathering up the materials he needed for the bomb.

He had been shown the process repeatedly and performed it countless times himself under his tutor's watchful eye. On August 2, he did it again, carefully assembling the explosive device in the comfort of his hotel room.

Only this time, something went wrong. Something terrible.

The newspapers gave scant details. Somehow the bomb had gone off. The room was destroyed. Juan Felipe died instantly. He was twenty-eight years old.

It took time to get his body home. He was buried on the 18th of the month. There were a lot of people I knew there, but nowhere near what I expected. I came home disappointed and dejected, and wrote a letter to a friend:

Dear Enrique:

I just got home from Juan Felipe Cruz's funeral feeling tremendously disheartened. The promotion this got on radio and in the press should have got the whole community to turn out on a Saturday. Three hundred of us went, all anti-Castro people who knew each other. The rest of the community rested from their work in the factories and went shopping. Even though they announced this was a hero of the exiles.

It was true. And it was sad. A twenty-eight-year-old man—a boy still, really—was dead. He had given his life for Cuba. For them. So that the friends and families they had left behind on the island could live free. So that they could go home again, if they wanted, to be with them.

And they couldn't even give up a couple of hours on a Saturday to thank him.

SOON, THOUGH, I too was focused on other things. As my trial drew closer, my attorney had more questions. He went through the government's accusations with me, point by point.

I couldn't believe what I was hearing.

Augustin Barres had been arrested in New York. He began cooperating immediately. He said he had put up the money for the drugs. I arranged the shipment. One of his employees, Ariel Pomares, arranged the sale here.

The way it worked, Barres said, was that I would go to Bolivia, buy the drugs, then give them to Bolivian diplomats who brought them into the United States.

Barres elaborated at the trial. He said he had met me in 1970, while I was organizing the assassination attempt against Castro in Chile. He said we stayed in touch, and did business together after I moved to Puerto Rico. He also said that many people in Puerto Rico told him I was with the CIA. Barres said he hadn't wanted to get involved, at first, but I had convinced him to do it.

I remember thinking how curious it was that someone would conspire to smuggle drugs with someone they thought worked for the government—especially someone with the CIA.

Barres said more. He said there had been three successful shipments before the one where he was arrested, dealing with the undercover agents.

I said nothing.

I was convicted on all three counts on January 14, 1974. The judge sentenced me to two concurrent terms of seven years, plus three years of probation.

We stood as he left the courtroom. Then my attorney turned to me. "Are you OK?" he asked.

"No," I said. "I'm innocent. I don't want my children to think I'm not."

He said that there was a possibility we could appeal.

"It's a long shot," he said. "But we might be able to convince an appellate judge to overturn the conviction, by showing that they made a mistake."

"They did make a mistake," I said. "I'm innocent."

WE APPEALED. WE lost.

They sent me to the federal penitentiary in Atlanta. They give you a rulebook when you get there. They give you a uniform. They give you a cell.

People ask me all the time what it was like. They almost always have an intensely expectant look on their face, or a soft, compassionate one—like they're expecting to hear about gangs and fights and terrifying nights. I think they see too many movies. The truth is, if you mind your own business, it's mostly just boring. The days all seem the same, and you just wait for them to end. That's what I did. I read, and I waited, and I tried to understand how an innocent man could end up behind bars.

Later, after my sentence was done, my friend Gaeton Fonzi once asked me, "Why didn't you take the stand? At trial. Why didn't you tell your story, and try to prove your innocence?"

I showed him a letter I had written to the presiding judge in the case, Dudley Bonsal, after I got out of prison.

"I did not testify during the trial for fear that something could happen to my family," I wrote, "because several 'political agencies' of this country wish to keep me quiet."

I explained to Fonzi that I waited until after I got out of prison to send it, so that the judge would know that I wasn't trying to say I was innocent so that he'd set me free. I was trying to tell him I was innocent because I was.

I don't remember if I told Fonzi about an odd coincidence I had noticed in the case. Judge Bonsal came from a prominent and successful family. He was a respected federal judge. His brother had been the U.S. ambassador to Cuba, while I was working with Bishop.

I WAS SENTENCED to seven years. They released me after twenty-six months. I got home in February 1976, just as the House Select Committee on Assassinations was beginning its work. Soon after my return, committee investigator Gaeton Fonzi started calling my house, asking to see me. We met for the first time at the beginning of March. He didn't mention the Kennedy assassination. He said he wanted to ask about connections between groups like Alpha 66 and U.S. intelligence agencies.

I ended up telling him about Bishop. The whole story. About Cuba and the attempt to kill Castro with the bazooka, about Bishop telling me to found Alpha 66, about Chile. And I told him about meeting Lee Harvey Oswald.

Gaeton tried not to look surprised. He tried not to let his excitement show in his voice. But as he himself told it later, "In my mind, I fell off my chair."

That's because he hadn't been fully honest with me when he introduced himself. He *was* investigating links between anti-Castro groups and the CIA. That was true. But he was actually interested in the assassination. As an HSCA investigator, he was precisely charged with looking into whether U.S. intelligence agencies had anything to do with Kennedy's death.

And I had just given him the thing so many suspected, and so many feared, but no one had found before—a direct link between a significant CIA figure and John Kennedy's alleged assassin, or at least the "patsy" for the crime, as Oswald called himself.

More than a decade had passed since the first commission to investigate Kennedy's assassination had issued its report. That one, the Warren Commission, was born within days of the president's death. Its purpose was ostensibly to get to the bottom of what happened. To find the truth. But its principal purpose was political—to quash any conspiracy theories before they cropped up.

It failed miserably.

The Warren Report only stirred up more troubling questions and heated debate. Matters got worse with the release of the famed Zapruder film in 1975. That amateur movie clip had captured the crucial seconds when President Kennedy was struck by gunfire in Dealey Plaza. Since the home movie showed JFK recoiling violently backward from a shot that struck him in the head, it seemed to clearly indicate this shot was fired from somewhere in front of the president's limousine, such as the infamous grassy knoll, instead of the Texas State Book Depository to the rear, where Oswald allegedly had set up his sniper's lair. This meant that more than one sniper was involved in the fatal attack on the president. The shocking Zapruder film soon spawned questions and conspiracy theories.

With public trust plummeting, once again the government created a commission, the House Select Committee on Assassinations.

Fonzi certainly had the right credentials to work for the committee. He was an award-winning investigative journalist who seized on subjects tenaciously and seemed to have an inexhaustible thirst for the truth. He had a long-time interest in the Kennedy case, and as the committee began its work, he became increasingly interested in the CIA's anti-Castro intrigue as a potential source of the plot.

"We called him Ahab, because he was so single-minded about that white whale," the committee's staff director and chief counsel, G. Robert Blakey, told the *New York Times*.

Fonzi's interest in the Kennedy case reached back nearly a decade, when, as a writer for *Philadelphia Magazine*, he interviewed future United States Senator Arlen Specter, who as a young staff attorney for the Warren Commission had developed the controversial "single-bullet theory" to explain how Kennedy could have been killed by a lone sniper firing with a faulty bolt-action rifle from the rear.

"It is difficult to believe the Warren Commission Report is the truth," the article began. "Arlen Specter knows it."

Fonzi hadn't gone to the interview expecting to arrive at that conclusion. But over the course of nearly four hours of interviews, he was stunned by Specter's stumbling inability to defend some of the basic premises of the "magic-bullet theory" around which the Warren Commission wrapped its final findings.

Though Fonzi had broken in as a journalist in Philadelphia, by the time Congress reopened the Kennedy case, he was living in Florida—and he knew Miami. He turned up at my door chasing questions about Cuban exiles because they kept turning up in strange tangential associations with elements of Kennedy's assassination. Others were doing the same with the names of various Mafia figures, including Florida godfather Santo Trafficante, Jr., the mob boss Jack Ruby reportedly visited while he wallowed in a Havana jail.

Now, sitting in my living room, he had just heard me give evidence that indicated there might be truth to one of the most explosive conspiracy theories about Dallas—that the CIA was somehow involved in John F. Kennedy's murder.

My recollection of the meeting between Bishop and Oswald flew in the face of CIA Director John McCone's sworn Warren Commission testimony that "Lee Harvey Oswald was never associated or connected, directly or indirectly, in any way whatsoever with the agency."

Fonzi would spend much of the next three years questioning me, pursuing the clues I provided him, doggedly attempting to prove or disprove what my simple statement suggested. In the end, he found ways to corroborate nearly every single detail of that meeting in the lobby of the Dallas skyscraper. At the heart of Fonzi's investigation was his effort to determine the true identity of the man whom I knew as Maurice Bishop.

I had never known Bishop's real name. In fact, he never actually said he worked for the CIA. When Fonzi checked, the agency could find no record that it ever employed a Maurice Bishop.

That didn't stop Fonzi. He took me to a police sketch artist to produce a detailed drawing of Bishop he could use in his search. Ultimately, it was Senator Richard Schweiker of Pennsylvania—the man who, along with Senator Gary Hart, had originally reopened the Pandora's Box of the Kennedy assassination while serving with the Church Committee—who told Fonzi that the image reminded him of David Atlee Phillips.

Fonzi's research found interesting parallels between Philips's career in the CIA and the places and events in my story. Phillips had been in Havana when Castro took over. He had been directly involved in the Radio Swan propaganda operation and the Bay of Pigs, and had risen swiftly through the ranks as chief of covert action in Mexico City, then chief of Cuban operations, and finally as the agency's Western Hemisphere chief before retiring. He had overseen Cuba, Bolivia, and Chile, at all the right times.

To be sure that "Bishop" was indeed Phillips, though, Fonzi took me to Washington, D.C., to meet Phillips face-to-face. We would be meeting at a gathering of the Association of Former Intelligence Officers, which Phillips had founded in 1975 after retiring from the agency. Phillips didn't know I was coming.

When we met, Phillips acted like he didn't know me. But I knew him. It was Bishop, my CIA case officer. I didn't tell Fonzi, though, and I didn't challenge Phillips right there.

Fonzi introduced us.

I switched to Spanish. I asked Phillips if he had been in Havana in 1960. Phillips, in Spanish, said yes. Did he know Julio Lobo? Yes. Rufo López Fresquet? Yes.

"What was your name again?" Phillips asked.

"Antonio Veciana."

"Veciana?" Phillips repeated, as if he couldn't quite place me.

"Don't you know my name?"

As Fonzi described the encounter later in his book, "Philips shook his head slowly and, with apparent thoughtfulness, said, 'no.'"

Phillips dedicated more than fifty pages of his memoir to his days dealing with Cuba. He waxed rhapsodic about his time on the island, about El Floridita, the watering hole for Hemingway and other Havana habitués, and a lengthy conversation he had there with El Che. He talked about needing to leave the island, and about continuing to receive intelligence reports from there after he left in preparation for the Bay of Pigs. He talked about the exiles in Miami.

But he never mentioned me once.

And now he was standing right in front of me, insisting he didn't even know my name.

"It's strange he didn't know my name," I told Fonzi after the encounter with Phillips. "I was very well known."

"That's funny," Fonzi wrote, "because I was thinking exactly the same thing."

EVENTUALLY, BOTH PHILLIPS and I testified before the HSCA, under oath. I told the committee my story and answered their questions as honestly as I could.

Phillips had many interesting answers to their questions, several of which led Fonzi to doubt his credibility. One was about the attempts to kill Castro. It was a story that Philips himself later recounted in his own book. And by the time that the HSCA investigation began, these plots were well known. The Church Committee had already revealed CIA plans to poison Fidel Castro with a hypodermic needle hidden in a ballpoint pen, to lace his microphone with a psychedelic drug to send him off on a hallucinogenic rant, and to expose him to a depilatory to make his beard fall out. Other plots involved booby-trapped conch shells and exploding cigars. They seemed inspired by spy novels and Hollywood screenplays.

Yet, Phillips, who had been involved with Cuba throughout much if not most of his career, claimed not to know about a single anti-Castro plot.

Phillips addressed his lack of credibility on this point in his book: "I have often been asked how it was possible that I did not know the Castro assassination schemes. The question is usually predicated on the assumption that when I became chief of Cuban operations and then head of all Latin American affairs someone would've told me, or I would've read about the endeavors and documents in my safe. The fact is that those few CIA officers involved did not discuss their participation even with senior officers not in the chain of command at the time of the plots. And highly sensitive papers are not retained in a division chief's office." Which sounds plausible . . . except I knew the truth.

For my own reasons at the time, I chose not to expose Phillips's lies. I never told Fonzi that Phillips was Bishop. And I didn't identify Phillips when I was asked about Bishop's identity under oath by the committee.

Nonetheless, Fonzi suspected the truth. He asked me again and again. He came up with his own explanation for why he thought I was withholding the truth.

"I was now absolutely certain I knew the reason that Veciana would not identify David Atlee Phillips as Maurice Bishop . . ." he wrote. "Veciana believed that Bishop was behind his being set up on the drug conspiracy charge. It was Bishop's way of trying to put a halt to Veciana's continuing renegade efforts to assassinate Castro."

Fonzi concluded that I was using him and the HSCA as "a shield against another set up. He decided to reveal just enough to let Bishop and the Agency know that if they continued to play dirty games with him, he would now have a weapon with which to fight back—the threat of Congressional and public exposure."

Fonzi was a brilliant and perceptive investigative journalist. I came to think of him as my friend. But when he asked me if Bishop was really David Atlee Phillips, I told him no. I felt bad lying to my friend, but he could only guess at the stakes involved when it came to breaking my vow of silence.

"There was no need to take his revelations beyond the existence of a Maurice Bishop," he wrote. "Veciana had nothing more to gain by identifying who Bishop really was—and perhaps a lot to lose."

chapter 11
A BASEBALL BOMB AND BULLETS

BEFORE THE HOUSE Select Committee on Assassinations finished its work, someone tried to silence me. With a bullet.

I had testified in secret before a congressional panel. I told them about the assassination attempts against Castro and about El Che's diary. I told them about Alpha 66 and about Oswald. And I told them how a man I knew only as Maurice Bishop had been responsible for it all.

Fonzi and other committee investigators were able to confirm much of what I told them. The committee had also determined that, even though the CIA insisted I had never been one of its operatives, the agency's records contained a "piece of arguably contradictory evidence—a record of $500 in operational expenses, given to Veciana by a person with whom the CIA had maintained a long-standing operational relationship."

The HSCA also strongly doubted the agency when it "insisted that it did not at any time assign a case officer to Veciana." That did not seem credible, according to the committee's final report, since I "was the dominant figure in an extremely active anti-Castro organization. The committee established that the CIA assigned case officers to Cuban revolutionaries of less importance than Veciana."

More than a year had passed since I had sat before committee members in a closed room in the Capitol Building. They had asked questions for two days in a row. Then they had gone about preparing their report. Meanwhile, I went home to Miami, to work with my son in the marine supply business we had bought.

Then, as the summer of 1979 came to a close, Fonzi delivered a copy of what he called the HSCA "staff report" about me. The committee's final findings were due any day, he said.

Someone didn't want me around to see the final report.

I was driving home from work when it happened. It was a little after 7:00 p.m., and just starting to get dark. I changed my travel route between work and home often, as Bishop had taught me. But the truth is, there's only so many ways to get home, no matter where you're coming from.

As I rounded a corner a couple of blocks from my house, I noticed a light brown station wagon. It was parked about three houses up the block, facing me. It had tinted windows, but I noticed a lone figure inside. Then I heard a loud popping noise, and I felt like I'd been punched in the side of the head. Hard. Then the vent window exploded.

That's when I realized what was happening. Someone was spraying my pickup truck with bullets. Someone was trying to kill me.

A third shot ripped through the door, chest high. Luckily, it ricocheted off the metal inside. Instead of tearing into my ribs, it veered a life-saving couple of inches. That bullet scorched across my stomach and right arm, leaving a searing trail in my flesh before it tore through the door on the other side and off into a field. Another shot cracked the windshield.

I hit the gas and raced for home. Nobody followed.

At the hospital, they told me how lucky I was. The shooter wasn't very good. And I had a hard head.

Police said the gunman used a .45-caliber weapon with a silencer. The first shot had come through the side mirror, splintering on its way through. A piece of it had been what hit me. It lodged above my left ear.

My wife said if it had gone any higher, I might have to wear a toupee.

The doctors said the bullet that grazed my belly was the one that could have killed me.

"You're lucky they used a .45," one of the cops told me. "The .45 comes out of the barrel slower. If they had used a 9 mm you'd be dead."

It's probably easy to suspect Bishop and the CIA. They probably had their hands on the same assassination committee staff reports I did. They probably figured there would be a media storm when the final report came out in a couple of weeks. They might not have wanted to wait and see if the media would come asking questions. They clearly were not eager to see me tell my Bishop and Oswald story on national TV.

But were they so worried about what I had to say that they tried to silence me once and for all? I don't know. I think there's another more likely suspect than the CIA. Castro.

Before I got shot, I received a disturbing call. A source of mine told me he'd been to a meeting in Panama with some of Castro's agents.

"They're planning hits on several people," he said. "They've got a list. Your name's on it."

Why then? Why not before? Who knows? Who can say why a snake strikes when it does?

My oldest daughter, Ana, had recently begun working as a reporter for the *Miami News*. She wrote a story about the attempt on my life, and about how we had learned to live with danger.

"But fear?" she wrote. "Never."

She explained that as exiles—forced to leave their homeland because a dictator stole their freedoms—we had a great appreciation of the freedom that's taken for granted here.

"The fear we know," Ana wrote, "if it can be rightly called that, is the fear many others are not fortunate enough to experience.

"I fear that we may have forgotten why we're here.

"I fear that we have grown complacent and smug.

"I fear the satisfaction that comes from having three cars in the driveway and a chicken in every pot, and knowing we can say what we damn well please without valuing that freedom.

"That's what I fear."

Fonzi included her words in his book. I'm glad he did. She makes me proud.

I was shot on September 21. I got my chance to get even the very next month. I read in a newspaper that Fidel Castro would be coming to the United Nations headquarters in New York in mid-October. I had another chance to kill him—almost exactly eighteen years since my first attempt.

Fidel was scheduled to address the assembled body of the United Nations as the representative of the Non-Aligned Movement, speaking on behalf of the Third World nations that had rejected formal ties with the major powers. Security, I knew, would be exceptionally tight. In the end, it included two thousand New York police, plus the U.S. Secret Service. There would be no chance for bazookas or guns hidden in television cameras.

I had two ideas. One was to use a radio-controlled model airplane loaded with C-4 explosive—an early version of a drone. The problem was, Fidel was expected to stay at Cuba's U.N. mission in mid-Manhattan. I saw only a very narrow window of opportunity. He'd come out of the airport and go straight to the mission. Then, he would be driven to the U.N. for his speech, returning to Cuba soon after. The Secret Service was keeping a tight lid on his itinerary. They wouldn't even release the scheduled arrival time for his plane.

Still, U.S. authorities expected competing crowds of protesters and supporters at the mission. So, I thought if we could get someone in the crowd, we'd have a chance for an attack. I thought the best person for that would be a woman, to attract less suspicion. The actual remote-control operator of the plane would be at a distance. Once she was sure which car Fidel was in, she could tell the plane's "pilot," who would crash the weaponized aircraft into the car.

I could foresee problems, though. The woman would have to decide which car would be the target. Then, she'd have to communicate, via some device small enough to be hidden in her coat. However, she'd be standing in the midst of a screaming crowd. That made an error in communications very likely. Plus, there was the possibility of mechanical malfunctions. The more complicated the plane, the more likely the failure.

My other idea was infinitely simpler.

We'd put the woman in the crowd, with the C-4 explosive under her coat. It would be shaped like a softball and be equipped with an impact detonator. She's on the street. She has the bomb. She pulls it out. She throws it. It's simple. The blast from a charge that large would easily take out the car and kill Castro. And there was a kind of poetic justice to it—Castro the baseball lover being taken out by a pitcher.

I got the C-4 from someone I knew in Alpha 66. Back then, it was fairly available, in the right channels. I bought a pound for $2,000. But I wanted to make sure the C-4 was good and would serve our purpose. We needed to test it.

I was still on probation, so I had to be careful. I couldn't be caught with it. So I asked an explosives expert I knew if he would test it for me. He said yes.

A few days later, the FBI came to see me at my house.

"We hear you have some C-4," one of the special agents said.

Naturally, I denied it.

"Look," the FBI agent said, "we're not here to give you a hard time. We give you our word that we won't cause any problems for you. We're not here to arrest you. We just want the C-4."

I knew they didn't have any hard evidence, and I wasn't going to give it to them.

"I don't know what you're talking about."

"We can be nice," the agent said. "Or we can be nasty. If you want, we get a warrant. We get the C-4. We get you on a probation violation. And you go back to prison. You like that way better?"

We were on the front porch. The C-4 was hidden inside, maybe forty feet from where we were standing. Still, I was pretty sure that in the time it took them to get a warrant, it could be long gone.

The agent named my explosives expert. He said they had already got some of the C-4 from him. They just wanted the rest.

I knew he was lying. I hadn't given the explosives guy the C-4 yet.

I was right about being able to get rid of the C-4 before they could get a warrant. I was wrong about the explosives guy, though.

I thought he had been the one who told the FBI. It was his wife. Not because she liked Castro. She just didn't want her husband to get in any kind of trouble. When she heard what he was getting involved in, she went to the FBI. She thought, correctly, that they would come after me and wouldn't bother with her husband.

In any case, it became pretty clear that there was no way the plan would work. In all state visits, the intelligence services from both countries work together to avoid security issues. Once the FBI agents came to see me, I knew they would send word to the Secret Service, which would send word to Cuban G2. Once the Cubans heard I was planning something, they would either delay Castro's arrival, or postpone the trip entirely.

The day after the FBI came to talk with me, I noticed a black sedan with two guys in it sitting outside of my house. They wanted me to see them. They made it obvious. They followed me and let me see them doing it. It was a message.

Our best chance to kill Castro in years was slipping away.

I was still thinking about that when my daughter Ana called. She was excited. The *Miami News* was sending her to New York to cover Fidel's visit.

"I'll be just a few feet away from him when he arrives," she said.

"When he lands at the airport?"

"Right after," she said. "At the Cuban Mission."

I HAD PLAYED out the assassination plot in my mind over and over again. I had seen the C-4 thrown. I had seen it exploding. I had seen Castro dead. Now I saw something else, too.

There's a chance Ana would have been there when the bomb was thrown. There was a chance she would have been within the blast zone. There was a chance that, in my blind obsession to kill Fidel Castro, I would have killed my own daughter.

I thought of something my wife, Sira, always said to me: "Don't keep testing your guardian angel."

She was very religious. She believed strongly in that kind of thing.

I wasn't so sure. It didn't matter. Whether it was luck or my guardian angel, my daughter had been spared. That made me think about how much I had risked trying to kill Castro. Not just this time—in Chile, in Puerto Rico, in Cuba. How many times had I put my family in danger? And how many others?

It wasn't worth it. I decided then, I would try no more.

My secret life was over.

EPILOGUE

MORE THAN THIRTY-FIVE years have passed since Fidel made that visit to the United Nations. As I finish this book, I am eighty-eight years old. I have great-grandchildren. And I have eighty-eight years of questions, and of regrets.

I regret that I waited until now to tell the full story. I regret that I waited until more than fifty years after President Kennedy's assassination to tell the world the explosive information that I had about the case. Namely, that my CIA case officer, the man whom I knew as Maurice Bishop, was actually David Atlee Phillips, a rising figure in the agency. And I saw Phillips conferring with Lee Harvey Oswald in a Dallas office building not long before the killing of JFK.

I KNEW WHO "Bishop" really was the instant I saw David Phillips's photograph.

Why didn't I say so then?

I was afraid.

I believe there was a conspiracy to kill Kennedy. And I believe that even if David Atlee Phillips wasn't part of it, he knew about it. He had to. Why else would he have met with Oswald in Dallas, less than three months before the assassination? And why else would he have asked me to help him connect Oswald with the Cuban Embassy in Mexico?

Immediately after the president's murder, the CIA began trying to tie the accused assassin to the Castro regime—a bogus story that the agency still tries to peddle to journalists and authors.

I knew, too, that men who would conspire to kill the president of the United States would think nothing of killing me. So, yes, I was afraid. Even more than that, I was afraid for my family.

At the time, I frequently drove around Miami with my family in the car with me. Even if someone's intention was only to hurt me, they could miss. They had already tried to shoot me once, when I was alone. If Sira had been sitting next to me, the bullet that cut across my stomach could have hit her. She might not have been as lucky as I was.

A bomb would be worse. As I well knew, a bomb is indiscriminate. Fe del Valle Ramos died because of the incendiary bomb in El Encanto in Havana. That was never my intention. But the bomb only did what a bomb does. It has no brain. It has no heart. It has no conscience. If someone planted a bomb in my car, my children might have been with me when it went off.

So I kept quiet. I only said enough to let Phillips know that I remembered him introducing me to Oswald in the lobby of the Dallas office building. And Gaeton Fonzi was right. I hoped that it would prove two things—that I knew something very important about Phillips, and that I was still loyal enough to keep quiet about it. What more proof could Phillips ask for? I had lied about it under oath to a congressional committee. If Phillips, or the CIA, wanted to continue going after Castro, they had to know they could still count on me.

After that encounter at the luncheon for retired spies, I never heard from Phillips, or from any of his colleagues, again.

And once I had testified under oath, I had even more reason to keep quiet. So the secret stayed with me.

There were many times I wanted to tell the true story. Like anyone who has ever kept a secret knows, it's a burden. A secret weighs on the heart and on the soul. A secret clatters like a prisoner's ball and chain, a shackle waiting to be discovered.

Many times I found it on the tip of my tongue, trying to come out. Yet even after the fear began to fade, the time never seemed right.

But, in the end, I chose the right occasion.

In 2014—the fiftieth anniversary of the Warren Report, the official version of the Kennedy assassination that came under fire as a whitewash soon after it was released—I was invited to speak at the Assassination Archives and Research Center conference in Bethesda, Maryland. The weight of the secret had finally outweighed my fear. My children were grown and on their own. Phillips had been dead for more than twenty-five years.

I probably could have gone public when he died, in 1988. The danger, or most of it, I think, died with him. He was the only person I could have identified. The others involved in the assassination— because there had to be others—had nothing to fear from me. I was no threat to them. And, since I have no idea who they were, I have no idea how many are dead, too. Maybe all of them.

But to tell it when Phillips died might have seemed like I was dancing on his grave. Or that I was trying to get revenge. I wasn't. So I didn't.

Then time passed again, and there never seemed to be a moment that was quite right.

Until the conference. It was a forum dedicated to uncovering the truth about the Kennedy assassination.

And Gaeton's widow, Marie Fonzi, was scheduled to appear there. With her as my witness, I felt I could finally make public the secret that had been burning inside of me for all those years. I felt, honestly, that with her there in that crowded room, I was honoring her husband, Gaeton, my friend.

He had known all along. But now, with her there listening as I stated publicly what he had so cleverly deduced, I felt that he would hear, too. I had told Marie the November before, in a letter. But this was different. This was me telling everyone that Gaeton had been right. I had denied him that confirmation in life. In this forum, in front of a room full of people, it wasn't just me telling what I knew. I was telling everyone that he knew, too.

It felt good.

And yet, even after this moment of truth telling, I still have one regret that I know I will never be free of.

I've always felt great remorse that I gave preference to political matters over my family. I devoted myself to a cause, to Cuba. That is my nature. But that meant I dedicated much less time to my family than I should have. My wife, who died fourteen years ago, had to be both mother and father. Thanks to her, my children were able to get ahead in life. They were able to study, and to succeed, because she did what a mother should, and she did what I should have been there to do.

Do I regret fighting Fidel? No.

Fidel was a dictator. Whether he was a Communist or not, he was a dictator. And a dictator, someone who represses the people—their freedom of thought, their freedom of expression, their freedom of movement—is repulsive to me. It's in my nature. And Castro, from the very first, showed signs that he was a dictator.

I had my doubts in the beginning. I wanted to give him a chance. Remember, what Cuba had been through before him, under Batista, was so bad, I believed that Castro had to be better. At least, I wanted to believe that.

But I knew a little bit about the history of Mexico, and Castro reminded me of the Mexican President Porfirio Díaz, a man who, in the name of revolution, became a dictator. I thought Castro was the Porfirio Díaz of Cuba.

Then he proved that he was.

His government has always imposed itself on the people through force. It used fear and intimidation to turn Cuba into a prison, with government guards and a system of trustees to keep the population in line.

There are those—mostly people who have never lived in Cuba—who defend Castro. They want me to admit that the Revolution did some good, too.

I admit it. Even when a country's leaders are perverse or evil, there's always something that they might do well. Fidel made it possible for many people who hadn't been able to study to get university educations. The regime provided education to all, and practically eliminated illiteracy. It did much the same with health care on the island, extending benefits to everyone.

Those are things that need to be recognized and accepted. He did it.

But at what cost?

Is the prisoner happier because he has free health care? Or would he rather be free?

I believe in freedom. That is why I fought for a free Cuba.

I don't regret that. I was very hurt by what was happening in my country, so I did what I thought had to be done. And I think I was correct in what I did. But I believe that I abandoned my family for a political mission. I stole those years from them. Politics consumed me and, in the process, consumed them.

And that I will forever regret.

BIBLIOGRAPHY

"2 Alpha 66 Boats Lost on Cuba strike." Associated Press, Oct. 30, 1962. http://www.latinamericanstudies.org/belligerence/Alpha-66-1962-1979.pdf

Anderson, Jon Lee, *Che Guevara: A Revolutionary Life*. New York: Grove Press, 1997.

Berrellez, Robert, "True Picture of Batista Regime's Atrocities in Cuba Begins to Emerge." Associated Press, Feb. 23, 1959. https://news.google.com/newspapers?nid=1338&dat=19590223&id=NP1XAAAAIBAJ&sjid=O_cDAAAAIBAJ&pg=2501,4729775&hl=en

Bowdler, Willaim G., "Memorandum From William G. Bowdler of the National Security Council Staff to President Johnson in Texas." Washington, Aug. 2, 1968. *Office of the Historian, Bureau of Public Affairs, United States Department of State*. https://history.state.gov/historicaldocuments/frus1964-68v31/d178#fn:1.3.2.1.10.47.4.6

Bundy, McGeorge, "Memorandum for the Record." Oct. 5, 1961. Kennedy Library, National Security Files, Countries Series, Cuba, General, 6/61-12/61. Secret. Prepared by Thomas A. Parrott. http://fas.org/irp/ops/policy/docs/frusX/256_270.html

Colhoun, Jack, *Gangsterismo: The United States, Cuba and the Mafia, 1933 to 1966*. New York: OR Books, 2013.

"Contra El Pueblo No Se Puede Luchar." *Bohemia*, Feb. 12, 1965. http://www.latinamericanstudies.org/belligerence/menoyo-confesion.htm

"Cosmonaut Will Share Top Billing With Fidel During Fete." Associated Press, July 24, 1961. https://www.newspapers.com/newspage/57522522/

"Cuba: every exile is an island." *Newsweek*, Oct. 29, 1962.

De la Cruz, Juan Felipe, "Ideario Politico de Juan Felipe." *Réplica*, Aug. 1973. http://www.latinamericanstudies.org/belligerence/delacruz-muerte.pdf

Fernandez, Arnaldo M., "The hit man and the mobster: Jack Ruby and Santos Trafficante." *JFK Facts*, Aug. 31, 2014. http://jfkfacts.org/the-man-and-the-mobster-jack-ruby-and-santos-trafficante/

Fonzi, Gaeton, *The Last Investigation: A Former Federal Investigator Reveals the Man behind the Conspiracy to Kill JFK*. New York: Skyhorse Publishing, 2013.

Geiling, Natasha, "Before the Revolution." *Smithsonian Magazine*, July 31, 2007. http://www.smithsonianmag.com/history/before-the-revolution-159682020/?no-ist

Gott, Richard, "Obituary: Antonio Arguedas." *The Guardian*, Feb. 28, 2000. https://www.theguardian.com/news/2000/feb/29/guardianobituaries1

"Guantanamo Assailed, Dorticos Tells Peiping Cuba Will Recover U.S. Base." Associated Press, Sept. 25, 1961. http://timesmachine.nytimes.com/timesmachine/1961/09/26/118519251.html?pageNumber=9

Guevara, Ernesto, *The Bolivian Diary of Ernesto Che Guevara*, edited by Mary-Alice Waters. New York: Pathfinder, 1994.

Guevara, Ernesto, *Congo Diary: The Story of Che Guevara's "Lost" Year in Africa*. Melbourne: Ocean Press, 2011.

Helms, Richard, "Memorandum From Director of Central Intelligence Helms; Subject: Statements by Ernesto "Che" Guevara Prior to His Execution in Bolivia." Washington, Oct. 13, 1967. *Office of the Historian, Bureau of Public Affairs, United States Department of State*. https://history.state.gov/historicaldocuments/frus1964-68v31/d172

Hoffman, Paul, "U.S. is denounced by Cuban at talks." *New York Times*, Sept. 3, 1961.

House Select Committee on Assassinations, *Report of the Select Committee on Assassinations U.S. House of Representatives, Ninety-Fifth Congress, Second Session*. Washington: U.S. Government Printing Office, 1979.

James, Daniel, *Cuba: The First Soviet Satellite in the Americas*. New York: Avon Books, 1961.

Kirkpatrick, Lyman B., "Inspector General's Survey of the Cuban Operation and Associated Documents, October 1961." TS No. 173040. http://nsarchive.gwu.edu/NSAEBB/NSAEBB341/IGrpt1.pdf

Kornbluh, Peter, "The Death of Che Guevara: Declassified." *National Security Archive Electronic Briefing Book No. 5.* The George Washington University. http://nsarchive.gwu.edu/NSAEBB/NSAEBB5/

Lesnick, Max, "Juan Felipe: La vida util y la muerte gloriosa de un joven patriota en Paris." *Réplica*, Aug. 1973. http://www.latinamerican studies.org/belligerence/delacruz-muerte.pdf

Mallin, Jay, "The World's Rawest Burlesque Show." *Cabaret,* Sept. 1956. http://www.cuban-exile.com/doc_176-200/doc0198.html

Matthews, Herbert L., "Mobs Riot and Loot in Havana." *New York Times,* Jan. 2, 1959.

Morales Córdova, María Isabel, "Un golpe donde más les dolió: el bolsillo." *Revista del Banco Central de Cuba,* 2011. http://www.bc.gob.cu/anteriores/RevistaBCC/2011/rev32011/canje.html

Pfeiffer, Jack B., "Official History of the Bay of Pigs Operation." *CIA, FOIA Collection,* Oct. 1, 1979.

Phillips, David Atlee, *The Night Watch.* New York: Ballantine Books, 1977.

Rathbone, John Paul, *The Sugar King of Havana: The Rise and Fall of Julio Lobo, Cuba's Last Tycoon.* New York: The Penguin Press, 2010.

Reeves, Richard, *President Kennedy: Profile of Power.* New York: Simon and Schuster, 1993.

Rostow, Walt, "Memorandum From the President's Special Assistant (Rostow) to President Johnson, Subject: Insurgency in Bolivia." Washington, Sept. 5, 1967. *Office of the Historian, Bureau of Public Affairs, United States Department of State.* https://history.state.gov/historicaldocuments/frus1964-68v31/d167

Suárez Pérez, Eugenio, "Nationalization means to put under the nation's control." *Granma,* Oct. 15, 2015. http://en.granma.cu/cuba/2015-10-15/nationalization-means-to-put-under-the-nations-control

Thomas, Evan, *The Very Best Men: The Early Years of the CIA.* New York: Simon and Schuster, 1995.

Vitello, Paul, "Gaeton Fonzi, Investigator of Kennedy Assassination, Dies at 76." *New York Times,* Sept. 11, 2012.

Walsh, Msgr. Bryan O., "Cuban Refugee Children." *Journal of Interamerican Studies and World Affairs* 13 (1971): 378-415.

Warren Commission, *Report of the President's Commission on the Assassination of President Kennedy.* Washington, D.C.: U.S. Government Printing Office, 1964.

"Yuri Assails U.S., Vows Soviet Help to Cuba at Rally." Associated Press, July 26, 1961. https://news.google.com/newspapers?nid=1917&dat=19 610727&id=aGUtAAAAIBAJ&sjid=q4kFAAAAIBAJ&pg=3426,365 1396&hl=en

ACKNOWLEDGMENTS

THIS BOOK IS a collaborative effort. Not just between Antonio, who lived it and told it, and Carlos, who helped him write it. They are both indebted to a small army of supporters and colleagues who made it possible.

IN ANTONIO'S CASE, that begins with a family that was always there for him—Sira, his wife, who unwaveringly shouldered the burdens of raising their five children, of working to help feed them and to keep a roof over their heads, and who never faltered in her love for him, or them, as he gave his life and his time to his cause; and his children, who remain devoted to their father even today, despite the lengthy absences, despite the thousands of missed moments of which childhood memories are made, despite the many times they were uprooted and taken from their friends, their schools, and even, sometimes, their relatives, and forced to start anew in new homes, new lands, and new languages.

There also are too many faithful friends for Antonio to name. Among them, a special, deep, and heartfelt thanks goes to Gaeton and Marie Fonzi, for their undying trust.

CARLOS'S LIST IS shorter. First, he wishes to thank Antonio for giving him the chance to tell this story, and Antonio's daughter Ana, who first brought them together. He also thanks the ones who suffered his sleepless nights and seclusion as he wrestled through the writing—Migdalia, Diego, and Olivia; Robert and Valerie for offering him a place in their hearts and their home; his tirelessly patient and dedicated agent, Greg Aunapu, who puts up with him; David Talbot, who made this book infinitely better with his depth of knowledge and surgical precision in editing; and Skyhorse publisher Tony Lyons for believing in this project and making it happen.

ULTIMATELY, THOUGH, THIS book is dedicated to the Cubans who have suffered, and those who died, under Fidel Castro, and to the dissidents on the island who are still fighting the good fight.

Antonio Veciana and Carlos Harrison
August 13, 2016